Second Edition

The
Address Book
of Children's Authors
& Illustrators

Corresponding with
the Creators of
Children's Literature

by
R. Howard Blount, Jr

Cover Illustration by
Peggy Jackson

Inside Illustrations by
Peggy Jackson and Terri Mitchelson

Publishers
Instructional Fair • TS Denison
Grand Rapids, Michigan 49544

▲▼

Instructional Fair • TS Denison

Dedication

To four dedicated colleagues and friends without whose support this book would not have been—

- Carol Field,
  Media Specialist,
  Tomlin Middle School,
  Plant City, Florida
  – a specialist in every sense of the word

- Carol Lane,
  Children's Librarian,
  Bruton Memorial Library,
  Plant City, Florida
  – a big kid's librarian, too

- Gloria Houston,
  Author-in-Residence,
  Western Carolina University,
  Cullowhee, North Carolina
  – genuine, literary, outrageous, respectable, inspiring, amiable—in excelsis deo!

- Martha Webb,
  Teacher,
  Tomlin Middle School,
  Plant City, Florida
  – a friend indeed!

My love and gratitude to you all.

RHB
Proverbs 31: 29

In Loving Memory of

Emily Cheney Neville	Jean Shirley	Elizabeth George Speare
1919–1997	1919–1995	1908–1994

Credits

Author: R. Howard Blount, Jr.
Cover Illustrations: Peggy Jackson
Inside Illustrations: Peggy Jackson and Terri Mitchelson
Project Director/Editor: Debra Olson Pressnall
Editor: Danielle de Gregory
Cover Art Production: Matthew Van Zomeren
Graphic Layout: Deborah Hanson McNiff

Standard Book Number: 513-02231-7
The Address Book of Children's Authors & Illustrators, 2nd Edition
Copyright © 1999 by Ideal/Instructional Fair Publishing Group
a division of Tribune Education
2400 Turner Avenue NW
Grand Rapids, Michigan 49544

▲▼

▲▽▲

Dear Readers and Writers,

We are pleased to present *The Address Book of Children's Authors and Illustrators, 2nd Edition*. Since the publication of the first edition five years ago many educators and young readers have been able to connect easily through written correspondence with the creators of the books they love. Little did we know at the time that our methods of communication were going to change radically in the next five years through the inception of the Internet. Although the primary purpose of the second edition of this resouce was to offer current mailing addresses of authors and publishers for traditional letter writing, we have included available e-mail and web site addresses as well.

The Address Book is divided into three major divisions. It would be very useful to read the **General Information** section in its entirety before corresponding with authors listed in the directory. This section tells how the book came to be, communicates exclusive, important messages from authors and illustrators to teachers, librarians, and children, and explains how to properly implement Write-the Author projects in the classroom or library.

The **Directory of Authors and Illustrators** is an alphabetized listing of book creators who enjoy corresponding with their readers. Each author page contains a list of titles selected by the authors or myself, a brief biography, the author's address, birthday, photograph, and direction concerning preferred modes of correspondence. When an author's address is listed as a publisher, please refer to the publisher addresses listed in the Appendices.

The **Appendices** contain masters for print and overhead reproducibles, various helpful lists, addresses and web sites of publishers and children's literature organizations, exhaustive bibliographies of resources for author studies, and general helps for teachers and librarians to facilitate implementation of Write-the-Author projects and other activities.

The intent of *The Address Book* has been to create a resource for teachers, librarians, and indirectly for students that would supply general information on how to correspond appropriately with authors and illustrators and provide an accessible address directory of writers and artists who will correspond with readers.

This book was born primarily out of a desire to put motivated students and teachers in touch with the authors and illustrators of the thousands of books they read daily in classrooms, libraries, and homes. I believe we have effectively facilitated that process on both ends.

Your colleague and friend,

Table of Contents

DIRECTORY OF AUTHORS AND ILLUSTRATORS

APPENDICES

An Open Letter from Johanna Hurwitz

Dear Readers,

In this book about corresponding with authors and illustrators, let me begin by writing a letter to you. When I was growing up in the 1940s and 50s, teachers never thought to ask their students to write to authors. Nevertheless, one day when I was about twelve years old, I felt so sorry to reach the end of the book I was reading that I just had to write to its author. The book was *Betsy and Tacy Go Downtown* and the author was Maud Hart Lovelace. I did not know where she lived or even if she was alive. Yet the very act of writing to Mrs. Lovelace and telling her how much I liked her story made me feel good. How did I guess that if I addressed my letter in care of her publisher it would be forwarded to her? I don't know, but that is what I did.

Imagine my joy when some weeks later a response from Mrs. Lovelace arrived at my home. The letter was a link between me and my favorite author. I read it over and over, and even now more than forty years later, I still treasure it. After that first success, I wrote to several other children's book authors: Lois Lenski, Alice Dalgliesh, and Dean Marshall. They all wrote back to me.

These days more and more teachers discover each year that writing a letter to an author is a good classroom activity or homework assignment. Sometimes, each child in the class selects a different author to contact by letter. Other times, the entire class writes asking for an explanation of something that occurred in a book that the class has read. Often they offer suggestions for sequels about the same character and even send stories that they have written themselves. Sometimes, they write just to say *Thank you for a story that I liked*. They send new drawings of my characters and drawings of themselves. And frequently in their attempt to reach out and connect with authors, the children send photographs of themselves and their families.

As an author, I learn a great deal about my readers from the letters that come to me: their names, their pets, their favorite foods, and TV shows. I have learned of the existence of communities in places I had never heard of before. Sometimes, a child will make me laugh by telling me a joke or asking a riddle. Sometimes, I will be saddened by a piece of sorrowful news that is shared with me. When my birthday comes around in October each year, whole classes send me birthday cards and sometimes they describe parties which they made in my honor. Even though I don't get a slice of their cake, I am thrilled to know about these celebrations. Later in the school year, on dark, cold February days, Valentine cards arrive from all over the country.

Sometimes, a teacher has reached the unit on writing *friendly letters*. Sometimes, the letter to me was assigned by a substitute at her wits end. Sometimes, children may want to tell me about something they didn't like in one of my books. There are many reasons why letters come to me.

Whatever the motive behind the letter, it is because of my remembered pleasure in the authors' letters I once received that I conscientiously answer every letter I get from the boys and girls, teachers and librarians who write to me.

I know that almost as soon as children post letters they begin asking their mothers if they have received any mail. Of course, it takes time for a letter to be delivered and a response to come. However, there are things which can be done to assure a speedier answer to student letters. Teachers should check that letters are properly addressed. Every year letters to me are delayed because a teacher mailed the envelope to a publisher's warehouse rather than the actual mailing address. Sometimes, I receive letters properly addressed to me but which have been written to other authors. It was the reverse of this sort of carelessness which made a fat envelope of birthday cards arrive many weeks late. This is what happened: A class of students in Ohio made the cards in early October. Their teacher placed them in an envelope and accidentally addressed it to Joanna Cole c/o Scholastic, Inc., in New York City. When Scholastic received the envelope, they forwarded it to Joanna Cole in Connecticut. However, Joanna Cole had recently moved from one Connecticut address to a different one. The post office readdressed the envelope and sent it to her. When Joanna Cole eventually received the envelope and opened it, she quickly discovered that the contents were really meant for me. So she put everything in a new envelope and sent it to me c/o my publisher, Morrow Junior Books, back in New York City. The envelope was then forwarded from Morrow to my home on Long Island. The well traveled cards reached my house three months after they started out. I was still pleased to get them, but what a waste of time and effort on the part of so many people (and a disappointment for Joanna Cole as well).

Just as my address should be correctly written on the envelope, it is equally important that students learn the value of clearly writing their return addresses. It is frustrating for me to receive in the mail returned letters that I have sent off because the address I had was incorrect or insufficient. For the student who has written to me but will not get an answer, it is disappointing. Occasionally, when I have the time, I have taken the returned letters to the public library and searched in the out-of-town phone directories hoping to find the correct address. But many children do not have the same last name as their parents, so this system does not always work. Besides, this is not my field. I want to sit at my desk and write my next book, not play detective.

Often during June and July, I receive envelopes of letters that students wrote to me during September, October, and November. Somehow, the teacher never got around to mailing them. Then as the school year drew to a close and teachers throughout the country were cleaning out their desks, the letters were finally posted. But alas, how can I respond? My letter will arrive after the conclusion of the school year. In September these students will not be in the same class. And even if they were, would they remember after so much time that they had written a letter to me? So teachers, please, if you are going to assign letter writing to your students, see that the letters are promptly mailed. That way you can expect a prompt answer and there is closure to the unit.

Despite the efforts of Howard Blount, not every author and illustrator you wish to write to will be included in this volume. Letters to others can still be written. However, to help prevent disappointment, teachers or librarians should help students check if the person is still alive. From time to time I am asked by children if I am friends with Louisa May Alcott or Laura Ingalls Wilder. This shows me that students are not aware of authors' ages and even the century in which some of them lived.

When my daughter was young, she wrote to the British children's book writer Enid Blyton. As it happened, the author was no longer alive. However, her editor at the publishing company wrote a lovely letter thanking my daughter for writing and saying how happy the letter would have made Enid Blyton. That response pleased my daughter although she was sorry that the author had passed away. Nowadays, editors are far too busy to take the time to write such personal letters to students. Usually, a letter to a deceased author or illustrator remains unanswered and a child is disappointed.

Sometimes, when students write to me they beg me for an answer telling me that the teacher has promised those students who get responses a special treat. Perhaps it is an *A* for the letter-writing project. Other times, it is a pizza lunch or some other gift. I always write a note at the end of my letter instructing students to please tell their teachers that this is not a fair practice. I hope my letter in itself is a bit of a prize for its recipient. Certainly, students who write to authors who are out-of-town, behind in writing deadlines, ill, or no longer alive should not be punished just because they didn't get answers to their letters.

It is also possible that the response that arrives to a letter to an author or illustrator will actually be a printed form and not something written in the author's own handwriting. When people receive hundreds of letters, shortcuts like printed forms may become a necessity. Otherwise, when will there be time to work on the next book? "Please don't let your secretary answer this letter for you," more than one boy or girl has written to me. I don't have a secretary, but the volume of my mail makes it essential that I write on my computer and not by hand. Similarly, illustrators do not have time to draw pictures for each of the groups that write to them. If you do get a quick sketch included in your answer, consider yourself particularly lucky.

Self-addressed stamped envelopes are always welcome. It is not that I can't afford to buy a stamp for your letter. However, no matter how many stamps I buy, I am always running out of them. Last year, I spent over a thousand dollars on postage stamps, and still I never had enough of them. If you include stamps, it makes life much easier for me. And another author who might not really have the time to answer you will see your stamps and as a result feel compelled to respond.

Howard Blount has made it much easier for students and their teachers to correspond with authors and illustrators. Read carefully his message about the value of letter writing. Then write your letters and address them carefully. I must confess that I worry about the increase in the number of letters that will come to me as a result of this book. Yet I promise to work hard to meet the challenge. For despite the burden of responding to the letters from my readers, I am always greatly enriched by it. The letters you receive from me and from the others whose names are listed here should enrich you as well.

All good wishes,

Johanna Hurwitz

Write Me Soon

By Norma Fox Mazer

When I was six years old I received my first letter from a friend of my parents named Charlie Dibner, who was an artist. Along the margins of the letter, which he wrote in black ink on crinkly white paper, he drew a few small, active, watercolors—one, I remember, was a cartoony me running to the fire station which was at the end of the street we lived on. I have never received another letter that pleased and thrilled me as much, although I have received a good many letters in my life by now.

I have always wanted to put that letter, or a letter like it, into a book. Maybe I did, in a way, in *Taking Terri Mueller*, when Terri writes to Leaf and makes little drawings to stand in for some of the words, beginning, of course, with his name. Terri's drawings are a world away from Charlie Dibner's, though. He was an artist, while Terry was my creation, and she had to draw the way I draw.

Letters have come into a lot of my books. In *After the Rain*, Rachel writes letters to her older brother. Originally, while drafting the book, I wrote the letters to find out what Rachel thought of this man who was so much older and so far away from her life. Then I liked them and realized that through them Rachel revealed her emotions in a way that was impossible elsewhere in the book. Several stories I've written have been cast completely in the form of letters. One book, *Dear Bill, Remember Me?*, received its title from the first four words of the epistolary title story in which Bitsy Kalman tries, over and over, to write a letter to her older sister's ex-boyfriend.

In life, as in books, I am attached to letters, although these days the ones I send often tend to be short enough to be called notes. Still, sometimes the shortest letters are the sweetest, especially when one is on the receiving end, as in this letter I found in my mail last week: "Dear Mrs. Mazer, I love your book, *Silver*. Please send me a list of all your books. Your fan, Amanda." With great pleasure, I wrote back an equally short and heartfelt reply: "Dear Amanda, I'm happy that you like *Silver*. I do, too."

I don't mean to suggest, of course, that letters should be short. Letters should be whatever length they need to be to say what the writer wants to say. In fact, letters shouldn't *be* anything, except perhaps honest. They can be funny or serious, zany or sober. Long or short. Light-hearted or solemn. Everything depends on the character of the writer, and the mood of the writer, and what the writer wants to convey.

Many years ago, Mary Wollstonecraft, a great letter writer herself, wrote to a friend, "Write to me soon and tell me you are merry and well—and then I will laugh and sing." Is that not lovely? I smile just to read it. In quite another vein, the English writer Evelyn Waugh wrote, in a letter to his wife, "I know you lead a dull life now. . . . But that is no reason to make your letters as dull as your life. . . . A letter should be a form of conversation: write as though you were talking to me."

Notice that, although he acknowledges her "dull life" he also believes that she can transcend it, that conversation—or letter writing—can be—perhaps in Mary Wollstonecraft's words—"merry."

"Write as though you were talking to me." What a wonderful charge, both for letters and for fiction. The thought that you can write as you speak might lift a lot of the terror of writing from everyone's shoulders. No need to use big words. No need to nervously ask twenty-five questions. No need to list the facts of your life as though you were filing a resumé with Heaven. Simply talk. Simply tell your story.

The way in which all of us understand, comprehend, make sense of and pass our lives is through stories. Our own stories, small and big. "I went to the dentist and . . . ; I crossed the street without noticing the light had changed and . . . ; I forgot to study for Mrs. Blassh's test and . . ." Sometimes of course, our stories are bigger, more sorrowful, charged with greater meaning and consequence, and they can't be told in one gulp.

The ultimate story, the story of our life is, of course, never fully told because we are rushing through it: being it and making it and feeling it every moment. But when we pause, we go instinctively to stories to bring to heel all those thousands of moments that gallop past each day like dogs or horses and which are, in fact, our lives.

And so what does this have to do with letters? Only this—letters too are part of the story of our lives. And kids writing to authors are writing or should be writing one of those nearly invisible pieces of the puzzle that is their own life. Tell me a story when you write, even if it is the briefest of stories: "I liked your book and I read it in only two days!" In that sentence is a triumph the correspondent feels. She is connecting herself to me, letting me in on a bit of her life. When she also adds "It always before took me two weeks to read a book," she enlarges her story, makes it more complete both for me and for herself.

I don't mean to suggest either that writers need only talk about the books they have read when they write to authors. Some of my most treasured letters from people who have read my books have barely mentioned them. True, it was reading a book that brought about the letter, but the writer had something else on his/her mind and told me.

Perhaps, most of all, in writing and in writing letters, we should all remember what the playwright (*Six Degrees of Separation*), John Guare said: "There is no one way to do anything." He was speaking of the differences in people, of how each person must write out of what she or he is. It is, seemingly, the simplest thing in the world. But, of course, the simplest things take practice. It takes practice to write the letter that is you, especially when you're in school, especially when the teacher is there at the head of the class, especially when you think there is a "right" way to do this, and especially when you might not even be sure who "you" are.

Try, though. Set out merry and well, write as though you're talking, and remember, tell your own story.

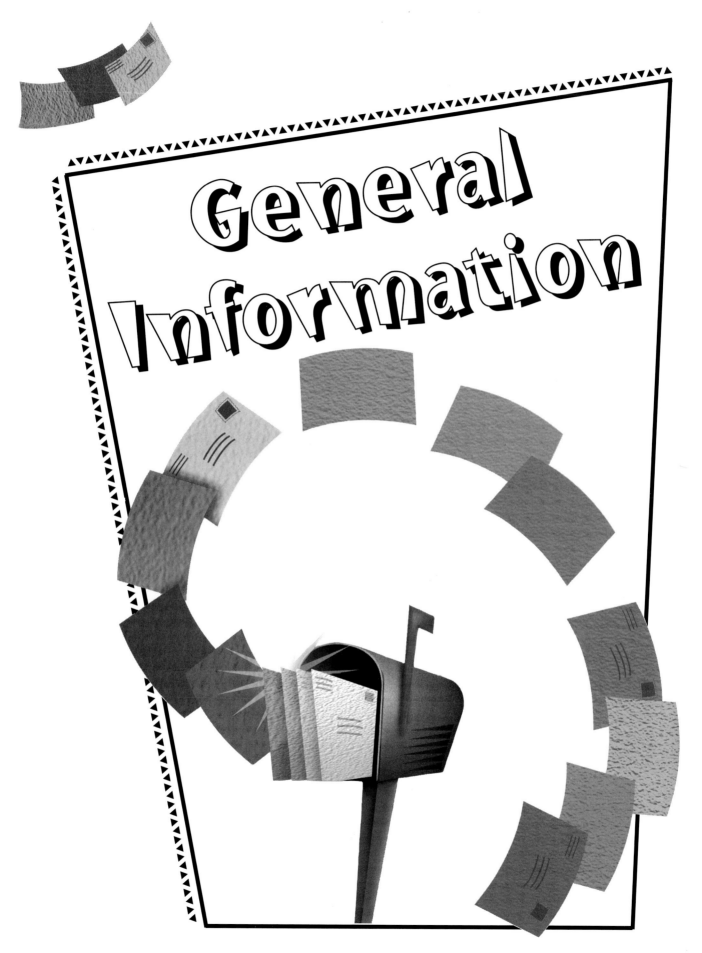

General Information

Corresponding with Authors and Illustrators—
My Journey

Note: Use of the term "authors" within the text denotes both authors and illustrators. Most authors and illustrators have been quoted anonymously.

The Problem

As a result of the trend toward literature-based curriculum, students, teachers, and librarians have begun to correspond more often with authors and illustrators. Unfortunately, this process has proven many times to be bothersome for all parties involved. Locating current addresses and the uncertainty of a response have created unpleasant circumstances for educators and their students, and responding to large quantities of mail has greatly reduced time and financial resources for authors and illustrators.

Published Letters by Contemporary Authors

It must be clarified early on that corresponding with authors is nothing new. In fact, several authors have published volumes of their correspondence with young readers. Such letters have been recorded in the books described below.

- *Letters to Children from* **Beatrix Potter** is a book by an author whose most renowned story, *The Tale of Peter Rabbit*, found its beginning in an illustrated letter.

- Theologian and author **C. S. Lewis** recorded copies of correspondence with young readers in his book *Letters to Children*.

- Lewis's peer **J. R. R. Tolkien** replicates letters that he illustrated and mailed each year to his own children in the book *Father Christmas Letters*.

- *A Letter from Phoenix Farm* is an open letter complete with many full-color photographs from **Jane Yolen** to her young readers.

- **Marguerite Henry's** *Dear Readers and Riders* uses many actual letters the author has received over the years to answer questions about the animal characters she so vividly portrays in her books.

- *Letters to Judy—What Your Kids Wish They Could Tell You*, a book by **Judy Blume**, also uses actual letters from readers who identify with Judy's characters and trust her with their most intimate questions. Judy responds candidly in this book for both parents and their children.

- *Dear* **Mem Fox**, *I Have Read All Your Books Even the Pathetic Ones* not only addresses the topic of corresponding with authors, it contains the internationally acclaimed writer's insightful, humorous, and poignant reflections on life thus far.

Undoubtedly, the correspondence between these authors and their readers was something beneficial, something compelling, something of enough value that it merited being shared with the world.

✎ The Quest for a Better Way

In the mid-1980s, a colleague gave me a card from a reading activity file that listed approximately ten addresses of authors who would correspond with children. We used those addresses, though I'm not sure how effectively, in my classroom that year. Later on, I discovered the *Something About the Author (SATA)* reference books at the public library which listed mailing addresses of most of the featured authors. Though *SATA* is an outstanding reference work, it wasn't always convenient for me or my students to make trips to the public library for the sole purpose of researching an address. There were many authors who, either were not featured in the series, did not include addresses with their listings, or whose listings were outdated. To correspond with those authors, some students wrote letters in care of publishing houses.

I knew there had to be an easier way.

Several years later my school district piloted a literature-based program, Total Literacy Curriculum (TLC), in several elementary schools. I was fortunate to be a language arts teacher in one of those schools. Though I had used novels in the classroom before, the training I received and the camaraderie I shared empowered me to create my own units and fall even more in love with literature and its creators.

Absorbed with the desire to put my students in touch with the authors of the books we so loved, I searched through stacks of catalogs for a resource book that addressed the subject of corresponding with authors to purchase for my professional library. I found very little. The various professional books I located contained only author profiles and activities. Though these were invaluable resources, they just were not helpful in facilitating correspondence. And they did not provide insight into the thoughts and feelings of the authors and illustrators who were drawn many times silently and unwillingly into the process.

Still, I believed there had to be a better way.

✎ The Research

I spoke with many of my colleagues, and they agreed that there should be some sort of resource book or directory of authors' addresses that a teacher or librarian could acquire for a handy reference. So, armed with the support and direction of several fellow teachers, librarians, an author friend, and the editor of a literature-based periodical, I proceeded to write and conduct a survey of the literary community to elicit participation in the publication of such a book and invite their answers to a wide spectrum of related questions.

I researched addresses and mailed questionnaires to over 300 authors and illustrators, with no idea of what types of responses, if any, I would receive. Almost immediately the replies started trickling in. I felt like a child on Christmas morning each day when I checked my mail. Like erratic precipitation, the mail would produce one day a drought, a deluge the next. I must admit, because I enjoy mail also, that the floods were best. Eventually it evolved into a game. I would try to predict the response to the survey by the size and thickness of the envelope and lack or inclusion of a return address. I got pretty good at it, but sometimes I was dead wrong.

The Response

Manila envelopes bulging with photographs, autographs, publisher biographies, bookmarks, and the like made for great mail. But the responses that gave the most pleasure were the personal letters, some handwritten, others typed, that expressed heartfelt sentiments and gave me great insight into the lives of some wonderful people. Hopefully, this book will effectively communicate those same thoughts to you.

All of the views the authors expressed, whether positive, negative, or ambivalent, ultimately came to be very informative and highly valued. Several authors apologized profusely for not allowing their names to be listed. Some approached the decision with trepidation. Others were extremely grateful for the opportunity to be included in the project. Most of the individuals, even some of those articulating a desire not to be listed in the resource book, returned insightful suggestions they believed needed to be communicated to educators and students, and many candidly stated that they wished there were such a book available. Their general feelings about corresponding with readers are probably best conveyed in the words of the authors and illustrators themselves.

The Regrets

"I'm sure that teachers and librarians will greatly appreciate your book—but I'm not sure that this author, anyway, wants to do anything that might cause an increase in reader mail. I would prefer not to be listed, at least at this time, although I appreciate being offered the opportunity. For whatever it may be worth, however, I'm happy to give you my thoughts and reactions to reader mail."

"I am almost overwhelmed by the volume of mail that pours in, although I very much appreciate the interest and enthusiasm that it reflects for the books that I write and illustrate. The problem is that some of the detailed responses expected would absorb all of my creative time, and if I complied, I would cease to function as an author and artist!"

"I'm sorry, I don't want to promise what I can't do already. I am <u>swamped</u> with letters. I love them, but the responsibility is great—not to disappoint, not to disillusion. But I do love the children, all of them."

"My dilemma is that working on books and speaking take up all my time. And though I always try to answer children's letters, the volume has increased to a point that I'm overwhelmed, and so I don't encourage mail. I, personally, feel terrible if I don't answer their letters promptly. I've found myself spending time on mail, when I should be working on the book projects—the reason why they're writing. However, I know from talking with other authors that they encourage mail and systematically respond. So, I wish you luck with your project. Perhaps I'll get to a point where, with a secretary, I'll be able to encourage mail, and if so will contact you to include me."

"I appreciate your invitation to be in The Address Book. *The fact is that I already receive a great deal of mail from children. Answering this mail cuts into my work time, and I don't feel that making myself more accessible would be in my own best interests. Those children who specifically wish to write to me can continue to reach me through my publisher."*

"I have had to hire someone to deal with the kids' mail; she uses a form response, and that's the best I can do at this point. I regret that, particularly when the letters are heart-felt, personal and genuine communication from children. Unfortunately, an awful lot of them are class assignments and somewhat perfunctory; those are the ones I wish we could somehow discourage."

"I hate to be uncooperative. I realize this is your baby I'm snubbing, and I do hope it works out for you and all the people who want to be listed. At my age, time is even more precious than it used to be. I love doing my books and being in touch with people who read them. But my days are already full to overflowing. I hope you understand."

"This sounds like a good idea, but I already receive more mail than I can handle."

The Paradoxical

"Of thousands of letters I've answered, one stands out. Or, actually, the letter itself didn't stand out to me, nor did my answer. But somehow my answer, according to her parents, changed this fourth grade girl's attitude toward school (she hated it) so much that she decided to become a teacher. The girl and I have been exchanging letters for nine years now, and next year we plan to meet. I don't want tons of mail, but if my writing back to most fans changes one life, my time is well spent." Ann Cameron

"Any genuine and spontaneous response from readers is treasured. Nothing is worse, on the other hand, than receiving twenty-five letters which all say the same thing, or which are obviously a class assignment."

"I do enjoy hearing from my readers, but the fan mail load is time consuming. Although I've had to issue a form letter—which most kids hate—I have no choice. I dislike having mail pile up as I believe every child who writes deserves a response. Often, I must hire a secretary

to address envelopes and stuff them. I could spend one day a week on mail, but this takes away from my book writing schedule. I don't like not responding to a child, yet, although I read every letter, I can't always jot notes or give individual attention. I regret that."

"I must admit my favorite letters are those which arrive in the summer when school is not in session. Those are the letters I am most certain were self-motivated and written from the heart and not because the teacher said they had to write a letter. Still, I believe there is value to be found in my responses to the students' letters whatever their motivation. And it is for that reason that I hope to be always able to continue answering them."

The Praise

"Your authors and illustrators directory is a good idea, and it will serve a useful purpose to authors and illustrators, as well as to librarians, teachers, and students, if you address some of the problems that are being caused by letters—problems of which the senders most probably aren't aware." Joan Lowery Nixon

"Good luck on your project. I think it's great to encourage the children to write. Many of the letters I receive are thoughtful." Suzy Kline

"Thank you for taking on this valuable project." Lynn Cullen

"You're performing a real service." Jerry Spinelli

"I hope [your project] produces an effect that will be good for everyone, authors and illustrators, teachers, and most of all, the kids." Marion Dane Bauer

"I wish you well and I hope your book sheds a useful light on the whole matter of letters to authors for many, many teachers and librarians."

"I appreciate your efforts at trying to alleviate this problem for all of us."

"I think it's a great project, and much in need of doing."

"Nice idea!" Betsy Byars, Patricia Hermes, Theodore Taylor

The Project

I do not know who responded more enthusiastically to this project, the teachers or the authors, but I do know that many educators and members of the literary community recognized the need for such a book. The final confirmation came when the editors at TS Denison, now Instructional Fair •TS Denison, agreed that this project should be in print. Believing necessity is the mother of invention, we are pleased to comply.

▲▼▲

Over 100 of the artists and authors who responded agreed to participate in the project and have their names, addresses, and selected works listed herein. This illustrious cadre of collaborators is an eclectic group whose creations cover every genre from picture books to young adult, fiction to nonfiction, and whose members range from prolific award-winning veterans to the recently published. We are eminently grateful to them all.

✎ The Purpose

This book is not designed to be a volume of comprehensive profiles. It does, however, include a brief biography of each author and illustrator to acquaint the educator and student with the individual and his/her body of work.

The intent, rather, has been to create a resource book for teachers, librarians, and indirectly for students that would:

- supply general information on how to correspond appropriately with authors and illustrators.

- tell how to write letters that encourage a response.

- explain the preferred modes of correspondence of individual authors and illustrators.

- offer exclusive messages from the authors and illustrators themselves.

- share what type of mail each person prefers to receive.

- tell what to expect in return.

- provide an accessible address directory of writers and artists who will correspond with readers.

- encourage beneficial letters.

If we achieve these goals, a formidable dilemma will have become a beneficial process.

▲▼▲

A Message to
Teachers and Librarians

Mr. Henshaw Speaks

So much truth can be found in the literature we read daily in our classrooms, media centers, and public libraries. Even the subject of corresponding with authors is addressed in the 1984 Newbery award-winning book, *Dear Mr. Henshaw*, by Beverly Cleary. The story of Leigh Botts is told through the letters he writes to his favorite author, Boyd Henshaw. Though the responses from Mr. Henshaw do not appear as text in the story, his responses can be heard in the ensuing letters Leigh is prompted to write. The correspondence begins when Leigh is in second grade, but soon he is in the sixth grade and his teacher has assigned a write-the-author project in order to improve the writing skills of her students.

The letter dated September 20 from pages 7 and 8 realistically describes the conditions under which most letters to authors are written.

- The teacher imposes a write-the-author assignment.
- The student writes only because it is required.
- The letter lists a multitude of pointless questions.
- The student requests free materials.
- The student demands an immediate response.

It appears that no real thought has predicated the letter. The student may or may not have recently read a book by the author, and if a book was read, there is no indication that it has affected the life of the letter writer in any way. The only positive note occurs in the first paragraph where the young correspondent alludes that the author may know who he is.

It is evident that the tables were turned on the young correspondent when his letter was received by Boyd Henshaw, prompting him to write a response of his own. The following letter dated November 15 from pages 9–11 alludes to Mr. Henshaw's response and provides insight into the persona of the author who has received the prosaic letter. Though this selection is fictional prose, several inferences can be gathered from the text with respect to correspondence between children and authors.

- Response time cannot be dictated.
- Authors do not live static lives.
- Authors resent long lists of irrelevant questions.
- Authors do not want to read unsolicited manuscripts.

- Writing unanswered letters to authors provokes anger in children.

- Assignment deadlines produce anxiety in students.

- Some authors return lengthy individual responses.

- Some authors write one letter to a group of students or a class.

- Single responses to groups can be duplicated.

- Some authors never answer.

- Most authors will eventually answer.

Somehow, page 1 seems to reveal that Leigh received more benefit, and more insight was gained by Mr. Henshaw with the initial letter dated May 12 that Leigh wrote while in second grade. Leigh simply tells Mr. Henshaw that the teacher read the class his book about the dog and that they "licked" it. It is signed "Your friend, Leigh Botts (boy)."

With the experience and first-hand knowledge that only a children's author would have, perhaps Beverly Cleary is uniquely qualified to communicate these thoughts to educators through the medium of a novel for juvenile readers published over a decade ago. Perhaps we should listen.

Teacher-Assigned Letters

"A single letter opened, read, thought about, answered, addressed—can take up to ten minutes of an author's time." Jane Yolen

By far, the topic that has received the most passionate response from authors and illustrators is teacher-assigned letters. The greater portion of the feedback I have received indicates that teacher-assigned letters are the least favorite, yet most widely used form of correspondence the literary community receives.

I guess if we were to imagine the bulk of our mail consisting of thousands of identical, individual letters written by people who don't want to write us, and we felt obligated to answer them, we might want to verbalize our thoughts, also. Until now, authors and illustrators have remained silent on the subject, out of fear of reprisals. They have had no voice with which to convey to the academic community their true feelings on this subject. I am sure they have heard the echo of the tiresome rhetoric, "If they want us to buy their books, they ought not mind answering our students' letters."

One author summed up the dilemma with these words, *"I would like teachers to understand that when they assign their students to write to an author, hundreds of other teachers across the country are doing the very same assignment. And unfortunately most authors I know, do not have the luxury of a 'personal secretary' to take care of the huge volume of correspondence that comes our way each month. (And yet if we don't respond, we leave fans disappointed and bad feelings are created.)"*

▲▼▲

I am sure many teachers and librarians are asking, "If we shouldn't use letters-to-the-author projects with our students, what is the purpose of this book?" Actually, the problem has not been teachers assigning letters, per se, but rather the way most letter-writing projects have been conducted in a misguided fashion.

I am not so naive, and neither are the authors, as to believe that with this eloquent discourse all teacher-assigned letters will cease to be. We just hope that somehow these words will be received and an improved working relationship between writers and readers will begin, and that in the long run, children will be the beneficiaries of the learning process and we the benefactors.

Many authors implored me to communicate this message to teachers and librarians. Through the completed surveys, comments, and personal letters I received, the authors shared their thoughts on how to improve the use of teacher-assigned letters in the classroom.

"I wish that teachers would be aware of the tremendous demands letters from children can make on an author's time. Writing to an author should be an optional activity for a child really enchanted by a book—not a required activity. I think children learn more doing research on an author in the library than they do writing me to ask how many books I've written, or my age. First, have the child do all the research possible on the author in the library. If the child then wants to know something more or say something to a particular author, then let him/her write. But don't push children to write authors! Also, I personally like letters that the child has proof-read for the completeness of the sentences, and that has all its words correctly spelled. It doesn't destroy a child's imagination or creativity to learn to be careful about details. It show respect for the receiver of the letter to do it right." Ann Cameron

"Thanks for the opportunity to vent some of my feelings on this subject! Like many authors, for me class assignments to write to an author have become an increasing problem. The problem stems from two main sources: (1) many individual letters (with home addresses) are sent from the same class (2) with no accompanying SASE. (In addition, children are now requesting a personal handwritten reply instead of a computer printed response! This makes any attempt at answering individual questions or giving advice almost impossible.)"

"All the [teacher-assigned] letters sound exactly alike."

"What I actually receive are a lot of teacher-assigned letters, written, not to communicate with me, but to please the teacher. As all good teachers know, teacher-pleasing usually precludes serious thought or creativity or even any real interest in the topic being written about . . . and it shows. Despite this, I answer all these letters with care."

"Why should children have to write if they don't want to? Why should authors have to answer?"

"I don't mind responding to genuine letters from young readers. But obvious class assignments do not deserve a response. They are simply make work. I also do not warm to the

open ended request for help on a class assignment. But comments, questions, and even criticism from people who have read a book are always welcome."

"I get tons of mail and some is so awful—the ones sent (or precipitated) by teachers. These often show that the kids just don't care but are being forced to do this by teachers (some of whom don't care either). The best, and most welcome letters are those from the children themselves, prompted by a concern of their hearts."

"I try to answer all the mail that I receive, and some of it is wonderful. But when writing letters to an author or illustrator is a classroom assignment, what results are not real letters, but schoolwork. There wouldn't be anything wrong with that, except that an equal or greater contribution is then expected of the author or illustrator, who is put in the position of basically having to put work into the teacher's lesson, or disappoint any number of hopeful children. I think I am glad you are preparing this book so that only those who want to be may be subject to this sort of thing, though I really don't think it is even ethical for a teacher to assign letter-writing. If it has to be done, one letter from a class would be an appropriate way to express that class' interest in the author. But I've gotten packages with thirty individual letters waiting to be answered!"

Several authors have stated that teacher-assigned letters do not present a problem for them, and not only do they believe that corresponding with authors is a valuable process, some actually enjoy every letter they receive.

"I very much enjoy receiving letters from my readers. My favorite letters are those that are spontaneously written, but I don't mind assigned letters either. I think, however, it is important for teachers giving assigned letters to realize that many authors are very busy and/or inundated with letters so not all of them can reply or reply as fully as the teachers and students would like." Marilyn Singer

"I do not mind receiving a package of letters from a class of students. I think it is good practice for them to write an author whose book they have read. It is not possible to give a personal reply letter to each student, but I do try to address all their questions in my letter to the class. Receiving fan mail is one of the biggest thrills of being a children's book author. It helps to keep me in touch with the feelings of children and their language. Also, I get most of the names of my book characters from names of kids who have written fan letters." Sherry Garland

"Personally, I love to get mail, and one way or another I answer it all. Feedback tells me this is much appreciated. I hope to continue." Jerry Spinelli

"I don't really have strong feelings about [teacher-assigned letters]. Some of the best work I've done is because I've "had" to do it. I suppose that's part of the nature of school, the workplace, one's career, etc. So, however a school chooses to handle this is fine." Helena Clare Pittman

"I've received many thousands of fan letters and look forward to each one! Each one gets my personal and grateful attention, and I've had the pleasure of answering them all. As an 'old-timer' in this game with thirty books to my credit I'm well aware that anybody can write a book—but nobody has to read it. I've got to make them want to read it! One of the rewards of this business . . . is the friends you make through the printed word. I'd rather hear from a reader than to prevent it because of some restriction." Ronald Rood

"[Teacher-assigned letters] do not present a problem if the content is not dictated."

"[Teacher-assigned letters]—not if they fulfill a need that cannot be met in a usual research manner, not if the assignments are well-designed and non-repetitive." Sue Goldberg

"I answer all of the mail which I receive. I love to hear from teachers and students, and look forward every day to reading the mail which arrives." Jan Brett

"If a child has gone to the trouble to write a letter, find an envelope and my address and a stamp, I'm flattered. I try to answer those letters personally. I feel that letters are a wonderful way for children to exercise the power of writing." Keith Baker

A Final Note

The participating authors have a lot at stake in this venture. A few have even indicated in their responses that they fear some people will abuse the privilege of having at their fingertips the addresses of so many literary people who are willing to correspond with their readers.

"I'm wondering if putting my name in your resource book will create more problems than it solves!"

"I fear your project will encourage kids to collect letters and paraphernalia from authors. If I detect this happening, I'll stop answering all letters. Please warn against it. If, on the other hand, your book helps children write to authors who really interest them it will have been a very nice service. Good luck!"

The purpose of this book has been clearly defined herein for the user. Rather than try to see how many authors will write back or see how much "stuff" we can collect, we must take advantage of this opportunity to evoke in our students a lifelong love of literature and learning.

Let's use this resource the way it is intended—

for the authors and illustrators

for the children.

▲▼▲

Implementing Write-the-Author Projects in Your Classroom or Library

✐ Benefits to Children

There are many benefits to be gained by children when they correspond with authors. With that thought in mind, many teachers and librarians use write-the-author projects with their children. Several of the outcomes that may result from the correspondience are listed below.

Corresponding with authors and illustrators has the power to:

- build self-esteem.
- give the pleasure of a response.
- teach the power of the pen.
- encourage reading.
- encourage writing.
- teach friendly letter format.
- encourage creative expression.
- facilitate being heard.
- demonstrate that letters are answered.
- show authors and illustrators as real people.
- motivate classroom sharing.
- provide a new form of communication.
- give pleasure in completing a project.
- create a sense of closure.
- " . . . demonstrate that writers are 'real people' and so de-mystify the process and possibly encourage writing by the children."
- " . . . deepen a reader's understanding of, or response to, a particular writer's work, or a particular book, essay, poem, etc., or writing in general."

✏️ Integrating Authors into Classroom Design

Reading is the primary focus of the language arts program in my classroom. My ultimate goal, more than high performance on standardized tests and more than gaining proficiency in writing skills, is that each of my students discover the joy of reading. I sincerely believe that if a child learns early on to read for pleasure, he/she will be able to learn independently the rest of his/her life. But reading cannot take place without literature, and literature cannot exist without authors. For this reason I design a classroom that lends itself to my ultimate goal. An extensive classroom library lines one wall, posters touting the joys of reading dot the walls, featured author centers consisting of mini-libraries, posters, and other information are displayed at prominent locations, while bulletin boards announce Newbery and Caldecott award winners and soon-to-be released titles. If the ambience of the classroom is geared for reading, you can be sure, as a matter of course, that reading for pleasure will naturally occur.

✏️ Author Studies

It is important for teachers to explain how books are written and illustrated by real people—that they do not just appear. To help present authors in this light, there are many commercially produced materials made available to educators. In addition to the professional resource books of author profiles distributed by various publishers, authors are featured monthly by the major children's book clubs. They vary in format from interviews and profiles to letters and contests. Author studies that usually consist of a taped interview, a poster, and a teaching unit can be purchased with bonus points from *Scholastic Book Clubs* and *The Trumpet Club*. Most publishers also have author biographies that can be obtained for a simple request in writing with an enclosed self-addressed stamped envelope (SASE). Author material is made available by organizations such as the *Children's Book Council*, the *American Library Association*, and the *International Reading Association*. Several fine video visits with authors are now being produced, though most must be purchased at substantial prices. Some videotaped author interviews are available from book clubs at discounted prices or for bonus point purchase. Educational and library publications frequently feature an article or interview with a children's author or illustrator. I hole-punch most of the information I collect and file it alphabetically with dividers in a bulging three-ring binder (see Appendices for addresses and bibliographies).

✏️ Conducting Research

If students are assigned research projects or reports on authors, they should exhaust the information that is readily available before writing the selected authors. The *Something About the Author (SATA)* series and many other reference works containing extensive background material may be found at most public libraries. Teach children how to locate information in discreet places like the flaps of book jackets or in catalogs. Make available the material you have collected, and show your students how to find and use the professional material mentioned above. If questions remain, students may write the authors or illustrators for additional information.

✎ Letters as Written Responses to Literature

At a recent writer's conference an author explained to me that he feared letters to authors were replacing the traditional book report, not that the traditional book report is not badly in need of replacement. He went on to explain that he preferred not to spend his time answering reader mail when he could be writing, thus the absence of his listing in this volume. I understand his concern, though I feel that letters to authors are certainly valid responses to literature. Should you use corresponding with authors as a written response to literature in your classroom, try to limit this mode to one per student annually. This will allow your students to experience a variety of written formats and not unnecessarily burden authors and illustrators with more teacher-assigned mail.

✎ The Authors and Illustrators Speak

The authors and illustrators who so graciously responded to my survey contributed extensive insight into their lives and explained from their perspectives how to facilitate the correspondence process. These impressions have been most effectively conveyed through their own words. . . .

"I think it would be very helpful if your book helped teachers and librarians to understand something about the life of authors and illustrators. Many support themselves with five-day-a-week jobs and write nights and weekends. Some of us are fortunate enough to be able to work full-time at writing or illustrating. With a few notable exceptions, none of us are rich or in a position to hire secretarial help. In addition to working, we have families, marketing, cooking, bill paying, all the details of everyday life to deal with. In short, we are not just idly twiddling our thumbs and wishing we had something to do."

"If letters-to-the author are going to be used as a class assignment, each student should, at least, have the opportunity to write the author of his or her choice. With this much element of choice involved, perhaps, more often, the letters would be fun to read . . . and fun to answer, as well." Marion Dane Bauer

"[You] may want to limit the number of letters to individual authors." Sandy Asher

"Limit the number of questions you ask the author to a few interesting ones. It's hard for an author to answer a lot of questions. Also, some questions are asked over and over and can be answered by reading the book's flap copy, looking in Books in Print, *the biographical material in this upcoming volume, etc. A teacher should suggest what questions might be worth asking."* Marilyn Singer

"I enjoy getting children's letters—when they are genuine to any degree. (Sometimes, it is obvious that a teacher has basically dictated a letter to a whole class of students who may or may not have read any of my books.) However, I try to answer all the letters I receive."

"Include a business-sized #10 SASE—it's almost impossible to use the teeny envelopes some kids enclose."

"It would be wonderful if students and/or teachers enclosed stamped and addressed business size envelopes for me to use when responding to them. Not only would this relieve me of some of the financial burden (50 letters a week X [33] cents = $[16.50]), but I am constantly running out of stamps. Also the time it takes to address each envelope further subtracts from my writing time."

"I never want to disappoint a child who has written, yet during the spring months, when teachers most often assign letters to authors and I often receive 40 or 50 letters just in one day's mail, my postage bill runs into the hundreds of dollars. Because of the expense, and the great amount of time it takes to address stacks of envelopes, many authors won't answer letters which don't enclose an SASE. I've mentioned this to a number of teachers. The problem hasn't occurred to some of them, but a few have told me they're not allowed to ask their children for even a [33] cent stamp. In this case, surely they could request a few dollars from a school fund or from the PTA, couldn't they?" Joan Lowery Nixon

"I appreciate it when a teacher takes the time to enclose a note of his or her own together with all the letters from the students. And I get annoyed when the letters are dated October, but the postmark shows me that the teacher didn't mail the envelope full of letters until March. What sort of follow up to a student activity is that?"

"The 'getting to know the author' letters rarely ask for information that would in any way enhance a child's awareness of the craft of writing or interest in a writer; they never reflect research done prior to the writing (e.g., use of reference works by child readers). They should!"

"Teachers should ask themselves and their students to think about the possible/ potential value of the answers they will receive: Why should I ask this? Does the answer interest me?"

"The teacher has the option of posting my letter for everyone to see or better yet, [photocopying] it so that each student may have his or her own copy."

"Please be sure kids put legible return addresses on the letters and envelopes. And please don't make assignments requiring immediate replies. That is often impossible for me to do. I travel extensively and often am away for a month or two at a time. When I return

home there will be stacks of important mail that must be taken care of at once, ahead of fan mail. If a child does not receive a reply it is because he did not give me a return address or I could not read it." Willo Davis Roberts

". . . I hate getting mimeographed letters asking me to send stuff, and I also hate getting letters from kids who are made to write them by their teachers."

"I receive many packets of letters teacher-directed and individual letters also inspired by teachers as classroom projects. Teachers set unrealistic goals for a response. Letters are forwarded by the publisher anywhere from one to two months after receipt of fan mail, and then must wait for my response, and yet teachers set a target date impossible to meet. Like other authors I'm sure, I receive requests for free books, both by teachers and students, on the assumption that authors have an unending supply. Authors' copies are soon distributed to family and friends. To supply free books, I must purchase them! And am also expected to cover the cost of the mailer and postage, not to mention the trip to the post office."

"By forcing students to write letters to me—and in many cases using bribery by having the student say that if I write back they will get a better grade—the teachers are asking me to do their job for them."

". . . there is no time to read stories or poems or manuscripts from readers."

"If the occasion is National Library Week *or* National Book Week, *teachers and librarians all over the country are having children write to authors, usually the better known ones."*

"Like all the other authors I know, I am always delighted to receive a letter from a child who truly wanted to write to me. It is a pleasure to answer such a letter. But I am far from pleased to receive letters written as part of a class assignment, readily identifiable by the form they take, the questions that are asked, and the lack of sincere feeling—and sometimes red-ink corrections and a grade. I see no reason why teachers should, in effect, assign authors to take part in classroom work."

"Don't have the children write letters to authors late in the school year—say, after February. I get letters very late and return mail is slow from Guatemala. If summer vacation arrives before my return letter, I think the excitement is gone as well as the child's memory of what he or she wrote me." Ann Cameron

"Please stress to the teachers the importance of having their students write clear return addresses. Furthermore, teachers should proof read these return addresses when letters are mailed from the school. It is very frustrating to me when I have taken the time to write a letter to get it returned to me three weeks later with a message from the post office saying there is no such address. And of course, it must be disappointing for the student who is waiting for a letter that [he or she] will never receive." Johanna Hurwitz

▲▼▲

✎ Points to Remember

The following suggestions gathered from the responses of the authors and illustrators appear to reflect the correspondence preferences of the majority. If we keep these ideas in mind when conducting write-the-author projects, the process should work well for all.

- Write letters to authors early in the school year.
- Remember national book weeks are busy times for many authors.
- Write one letter from the whole class, if possible.
- Batch if individual letters are mailed, and expect a single response.
- Enclose a personal note with class letters.
- Allow students to write to the author of their choice.
- Limit the number of letters mailed to individual authors.
- Verify that the child has read a book by the author being written.
- Encourage research prior to letter writing.
- Discuss appropriate questioning with students.
- Evaluate merits of individual questions.
- Qualify comments, questions, compliments, and criticism.
- Encourage candor, humor, ingenuity, originality, and spontaneity.
- Refrain from mailing letters with red-ink teacher corrections.
- Send original letters only—no photocopied form letters or dictation.
- Refrain from infusing personal agenda in children's letters.
- Refrain from setting deadlines for author responses.
- Do not send a guilt trip in order to encourage a response.
- Enclose a #10 business size SASE (self-addressed stamped envelope).
- Verify legibility of return addresses on letters and SASEs.
- Mail letters promptly.
- Wait patiently for a response.
- Photocopy single responses for the whole class.
- Share letters and responses in class.
- Conduct follow-up activities.

▲▼▲

I am sure some teachers wonder about sending book-related writings and illustrations from their students. The responses I gathered from the literary community ranged from "Love them!" to "NO!!!" If a listed author or illustrator enjoys receiving such material, it is mentioned on the author's page in the directory. If writing and drawings are sent, do not expect them to be returned.

✎ Writing Good Letters

Writing an author or illustrator should be a meaningful experience prompted by a reader's desire to communicate a heartfelt message. Even if the letters are used as class assignments, students should be encouraged to make them a pleasure to read. Instruct the children to ask themselves, "What letter content is most interesting to me?" Great letters should be:

• heartfelt	• insightful	• humorous
• candid	• ingenious	• spontaneous
• realistic	• evaluative	• original

Several authors and illustrators commented specifically on the types of letters they enjoy and the types they abhor.

" . . . *comments about books, relevant questions about the reader's interests and concerns, how [or] why book was chosen by reader, perceived significance of content. I like to get letters in which kids relate stories to their own experiences, raise questions, report how the story made them feel or challenge some aspects.*"

"*I refuse to answer a string of questions. In the letters which often begin, 'Our teacher said we had to read a book and write to the author' are usually a list of questions, not from the students' real interest but from a list obviously copied from the board. I keep an updated newsletter, which contains answers to questions I'm asked the most, and which tells something about my newest books. These are sent to the 'had to write to the author' letter writers.*" Joan Lowery Nixon

"*I always answer letters that are obviously reader-initiated (you can always tell the difference).*"

"*Teachers should check the letters for honesty (I have published exactly two novels. Don't write me: I love ALL your great stories!).*"

"*The most enjoyable letters are those that come straight from the heart with all the errors. Form letters are a bore!*" Patricia McKissack

▲▼▲

"In some perfect world, I would receive only letters from young people and adults who wanted to write to me because they had something they wanted, quite passionately, to say, positive or negative." Marion Dane Bauer

"Hopefully, letters would emerge from a classroom in the natural context of reading and studying literature." W. Nikola-Lisa

"I much prefer letters from individuals generated by their own interest." David Budbill

"(1) What I like the least: letters written mainly to collect an autograph. (2) What I like almost as little: letters assigned by teachers or letters that express the teacher's agenda or letters asking questions that make no sense . . . If a teacher or a parent is involved in letter-writing, I think some editing may be in order. I refuse to answer letters that show no genuine curiosity and thought on the part of the writer(s). But if a letter is sincere and thoughtful, I will answer it as thoroughly and lovingly as I can."

"A few years ago it became a fad to have students write, 'The thing I liked best about your book was . . . and the think I liked least about your book was . . .' Whoa! What about teaching manners? A letter to an author is not a book report. It's a polite form of communication. Authors are human beings with feelings, and kids—trying hard to meet the teacher's requirement to write something about the best and least, will often write some far-fetched negative statements that have nothing to do with the book. (There are always the darling ones who write, 'The thing I liked least about your book was that it ended too soon because I loved reading it.') Also, teachers need to read the letters they're sending out. They'd be surprised at what a student, angry at having to complete the assignment, can write." Joan Lowery Nixon

Topics to Avoid in Letters to Authors

Several subjects have no place in letters to the author—intrusive or irrelevant questions, audacious requests, or tactless comments. Adults and children should refrain from including the following types of items in correspondence with authors and illustrators:

- asking how much money authors make

- asking age

- sending food

- sending manuscripts for evaluation

- asking advice for budding adult authors

- long lists of questions

- letters that express the teacher's agenda

- coercion, subtle or otherwise, to elicit a response—*"Please send me all the free information you can on . . . and please hurry. My paper is due on Thursday."*

- rude comments—*"I didn't want to write this letter, we had to, it's a school assignment."*

- irrelevant questions—*"Do you have sisters or brothers? I have three."*

- intrusive questions—*"Are you married? What if the author is recently widowed? has chosen a lifestyle that is problematic in some communities? is in the midst of a difficult divorce?"*

- formulaic letters—*"Who invented 'Hi. My name is _____' as the opening, over-used phrase?!"*

- requests for free books—*"You could do authors and illustrators a great service if you let schools and libraries know that requests for free copies of books are not appreciated. Perhaps they don't realize that an author only receives ten free copies and has to buy any additional books herself."*

Whole Class Letters

When a book has been shared by an entire class as a read-aloud or focus title, students may be motivated to write the author or illustrator or the teacher may want to write a class letter as a follow-up activity. This type of correspondence may take one of two forms: a single letter from the whole class completed as a language experience activity, or individual letters from each child. Regardless of the mode selected, expect one letter from the author to the whole class in return.

"Whole class letters are often great fun to answer, and I've made friends with a number of classes who send large manila envelopes filled with letters. However, these are the class letters which arrive with a cover letter from their teacher in which I might be told about the classroom use of the book, the fun some of the students had in writing a play using one of the scenes, organizing a costume parade, or making an exhibit, and in which the teacher assures me that one letter addressed to the entire class will be welcomed. You'd be surprised at how many times I receive an envelope, stamped only with the school's return address, which contains forty to fifty letters, each with the student's home address. Even with a computer's help, that's an impossible chore to give the author. If somewhere among the letters one of the young writers mentions the name of the teacher, I write a letter to the class, addressed to the teacher. If there are no clues I have to discard the letter, unanswered." Joan Lowery Nixon

"When a number of kids from the same class write letters, I'd rather they be sent as all one batch instead of mailed in individual envelopes. Sometimes I imagine teachers have their students do it that way in order to prompt individual responses from the author. They just don't seem to realize the volume of mail that can come in and that, on a day in which

several such batches arrive, it's literally impossible to answer 25 letters each from a number of classes. The answer, form at least, is one reply in answer to a batch." Jerry Spinelli

"With over 1000 letters coming in per month, class letter writing assignments (those that arrive one letter at a time, over a 2–3 week period) usually don't get responses."

"If an entire class has enjoyed a book together, it's most helpful to me if they discuss what they liked or disliked most, and then write a single letter together, rather than send a thick envelope filled with 30 letters." Phyllis Reynolds Naylor

"Most batches of 30 in a envelope are answered with one letter." Sandy Asher

Individual Letters

When assigning letters to the author, it is very important that each child be given the latitude to select which author to write. The letter should be written soon after the book has been read so that the content will fresh in the child's mind. Should you choose to make this a requirement that may be completed at any time during the year, it will be helpful to keep a record of student correspondence. A generic checklist has been included for your convenience (see Appendices). However you choose to implement the project, remember not to set deadlines for authors to respond, and refrain from giving the child a grade for the author's work.

Keeping a Reading Journal for a Specific Book

"One of my favorite letters is five short computer-typed letters written as a boy read my book. 'Now I am on page—and I think Ollie is in trouble.' It was delightful. The creativeness of kids!! I can always spot a teacher 'suggested' letter." Barbara Steiner

Many teachers use reading journals with their students, assigning them to record their responses to literature periodically throughout the school year. In addition to journals, my students keep a single class discussion log where they record group discussion topics prompted by the literature we read. Any student may write in the log, and usually two or three children will write reflections on the same day.

Keeping a reading journal is one of the best ideas I know for sharing a reading experience with an author or illustrator whose books have been used in class. A journal may be used daily with several individuals recording their reflections from the reading of a class focus novel or read-aloud title. Or students in a class may each read a book independently, selected from a variety of authors, and keep individual journals for their own books. Independent reading journals may consist of inexpensively purchased composition books or handmade books created by stapling several sheets of notebook paper together and designing a construction paper cover. Students should be reminded that it is very important to record dates for every entry they make. If the journal is kept by a whole class that is sharing a book, it would be preferable for the sponsoring teacher to include a cover letter when mailing.

Writing Authors Who Are Dead

Learning of an author's demise is a sad thought for children who love and respect an individual's body of work. Children need to understand, however, that Frances Hodgson Burnett, Laura Ingalls Wilder, and Wilson Rawls will not be able to write them back. An associate of Holiday House informed me that they still receive letters for Jim Kjelgard, and I have had students ask me for the address of Scott O'Dell and other popular authors who are deceased. Teaching about the classics, modern classics, contemporary fiction, and their authors helps students better visualize the era in which certain books were written and published. Identifying the copyright date of a title prior to reading also gives young readers an idea of the time period in which the author wrote the manuscript. Writing letters to deceased authors in a journal, rather than for mailing, may be a suitable alternative for some children. Occasionally when writing contemporary authors a letter may be sent to an author who has recently passed away. When I was conducting the research for this book, I received a response from a widow whose spouse had died only a few years ago. I also discovered that an author I thought had died was not only very much alive—he wanted to be listed in this directory. Perhaps in cases of letters sent to authors who have died, publishing houses may be able to provide responses.

Teachers and Librarians Writing Authors and Illustrators

Teachers and librarians may wish to write authors to request background information for a title they are about to read with a group. They may also find it rewarding to share with an author samples of class response activities, cute student reactions to a story, or videos of plays, parties, and parades. Most authors who enjoy hearing from children would probably enjoy hearing from their teachers as well. Educators should remember, however, that the procedures children are expected to follow when corresponding with authors, plus a few more, apply to adults as well. Never put authors or illustrators on the spot by asking them to critique your manuscripts or sketches. Those services should be obtained by seeking someone who does that line of work for a fee. Do not request free materials for prizes or gifts, though it may seem to you to be for a worthy cause. Authors would have to declare bankruptcy if they donated to every "charitable" cause that was presented.

"We absolutely do not want to receive letters from would-be authors (adults) seeking advice. . . . "

"Even more outrageous are the letters asking authors to contribute prizes to be awarded to the students who have read the most books (or whatever)."

▲▼▲

*"There is one kind of mail I **do not** want to receive—manuscripts from aspiring writers. I have even had parents or teachers shove a manuscript at me after or before a school talk in hopes that I would read it and tell them where to get it published. There are hundreds of people who get paid for critiquing manuscripts and I feel it is taking advantage of an author to ask her/him to read such materials."*

✎ Teaching Letter Writing

I have learned the hard way to assume nothing when teaching friendly letter writing. Even at the sixth grade level, the lack of retention is amazing, and many children have never had the opportunity to mail real letters in their lives. Background knowledge in this department is certainly minimal in the average classroom. Through the medium of my own *faux pas*, I offer these words of wisdom in a preventative spirit.

When I was mailing out the author and illustrator questionnaires that precluded this volume, several of my students volunteered to help me stamp envelopes. One seemingly bright child thought the postage stamp had to be pasted directly in the upper right corner of the envelope. The result was a stack of envelopes with stamps hanging off the edge so they could be easily knocked off by postal service handling. Of course I knew upon receipt of the ill-fated envelopes, the entire literary community would identify me for the amateur that I was.

Another time approximately 80 envelopes had been self-addressed and tri-folded prior to stamping. I unfolded one envelope and gave the group a demonstration of how to complete the task. When they had finished, the envelopes were proudly presented to me with the stamps precisely placed in the corner of the center tri-fold. My reaction disqualified me for sainthood. I ended up soaking every envelope in water (steam does not work), removing the stamps, laying them out to dry, re-gluing them to new envelopes, and repeating the addressing and folding process. What a learning experience!

In addition to writing to authors, my students correspond with their pen pals, send thank-you letters when we have special speakers, and write various and sundry other letters to encourage global change. No matter how many times I review the friendly letter format and how many times we write letters, I always have children who habitually indent the greetings—sometimes halfway across the page. Should you discover the secret of effectively teaching this skill, please write me and let me know. I would be eternally grateful.

Letter-Writing Activities

✎ **Friendly Letters: An Introductory Lesson**

Equipment: overhead projector, screen

Materials: friendly letter format and friendly letter guide transparencies (see Appendices for reproducible forms), water-soluble marker, dampened paper towel, one copy of the friendly letter guide for each student

- Explain that a friendly letter is a written form of informal communication between two people who are separated by distance.

- Display the transparency of friendly letter format.

- Discuss the five parts of a friendly letter, explaining their purposes and rules of usage.

Heading – three lines of information justified to the right margin.

Line 1 – the letter writer's street address, PO Box, or RR
Line 2 – the letter writer's city, state, and Zip Code®
Line 3 – the date the letter is written

The first letter of all proper nouns listed in the heading are to be capitalized. Commas follow the name of the city on line 2 and the day on line 3. Never place sections from one line on the following line (e.g., placing the ZIP Code ® at the beginning of line 3).

Salutation – one line of greeting justified to the left margin beginning with the term "Dear" followed by the recipient's name and a comma. Use abbreviated titles before names when needed. The salutation is not indented.

Body – a paragraph or series of paragraphs that communicates the letter writer's message to the recipient. Each paragraph is indented.

Closing – one line of dismissal justified to the right. The first letter of the first word is capitalized while the following words are written in lowercase, unless they are proper nouns. A comma follows the final word.

Signature – the name of the letter writer. The signature must be written legibly unless the letter writer is known to the recipient.

- Replace the friendly letter format transparency with the friendly letter guide transparency. Review the five parts of the friendly letter, asking students to name them as you label them with a water-soluble marker. Erase with a dampened paper towel.

- As a class, write a practice letter to a fictional character on the friendly letter guide transparency. Review the rules of usage as each section is completed.

- Select a student to read the letter to the class.

- Distribute photocopies of the friendly letter guide to the class. Assign each student to write a letter to a classmate. Leave the class letter displayed on the overhead for reference.

- Share several letters orally with the class.

Addressing Envelopes: An Introductory Lesson

Equipment: overhead projector, screen

Materials: envelope format and envelope guide transparencies (see Appendices for reproducilble forms), water soluble pen, dampened paper towel, one copy of the envelope guide for each student

- Explain that envelopes bear both the address of the person mailing the letter and the person receiving the letter. Accurate legible addressing should ensure delivery of the letter.

- Display the transparencies of envelope format and envelope guide.

- Discuss the three parts of an envelope, explaining their purposes and rules of usage.

Return Address – the address of the person mailing the letter written in the upper left corner.

Line 1 – the letter writer's name
Line 2 – the letter writer's street address, PO Box, or RR
Line 3 – the letter writer's city, state, and ZIP Code®

Mailing Address – the address of the letter recipient written in the center of the envelope.

Line 1 – the letter recipient's name
Line 2 – the letter recipient's street address, PO Box, or RR
Line 3 – the letter recipient's city, state, and ZIP Code®

Traditionally, the first letter of all proper nouns listed in the addresses are to be capitalized, and commas follow the name of the city on line 3. Never place sections from one line on the following line (e.g., placing the PO Box number at the beginning of line 3).

The United States Postal Service, which delivers over half a billion pieces of mail daily, has issued current procedure for addressing letters to ensure prompt delivery. New facilities and high-speed electronic scanning equipment allow properly addressed mail to be delivered quicker than ever before. If you opt to use this most current method, remember these important points when addressing envelopes (see Appendices).

- Write using black ink.

- Print using all uppercase characters.

- Omit punctuation such as periods and commas.

- Use the new standard address and state abbreviations.

- Use the correct Zip Code® or Zip+4® code.

Following Process Writing Standards

Better letters will result if children follow process writing standards when corresponding with authors. The four main steps are:

1. pre-writing
2. draft
3. edit
4. publish

In the **pre-writing** stage, students reflect on the books they have read, jotting down questions and comments they want to include in their letters. With these notes handy, they write a **draft** of their letters without being overly concerned with spelling and punctuation. The **edit** stage may consist of self-editing, peer-editing, teacher-editing, or all three. At this point, some teachers may choose to insert an additional step for students to **revise** their letters, or rewrite them with corrections. When the students finally **publish** their letters, the letters should be ready to mail. Copies of the published letters should be retained in the students' writing folders or portfolios.

Other Activities

Several pages in the Appendices are dedicated to providing examples of letters and envelopes. The pages may be reproduced as handouts for students or made into overhead transparencies for lessons. The examples of the poorly-written letter and envelope may be used as a daily oral language activity. Direct students to address specifically what is wrong with each example and explain how to make corrections. Then show the examples that demonstrate good writing skills. Share the pages that list valid and poor reasons to write authors and examples of valid and poor questions to ask. The various checklists for students and teachers may be duplicated as needed.

Recording the Event in Journals

Encourage students to write journal entries on the days their letters are mailed so they will have a permanent record of this exciting activity. They may want to express their feelings concerning the project, make predictions of when their letters will be answered, or tell what they expect their responses to be. When the answers to their letters arrive, the students may want to record that event in their journals also.

Designing Stationery

Many children enjoy "decorating" their letters and envelopes with small sketches. This is a nice way for children to personalize their mail as long as their artwork does not overpower the content of the letters or interfere with the legibility of addresses. Prior to directing students to publish their letters, inventive teachers or librarians may want to execute art activities to create stationery by marbling, antiquing, or using stamp pads.

Return Home Addresses or School Address

Early on, teachers need to determine whether their children will use the school address or their home addresses for return mail. If the school address is used, the teacher will be able to verify when students receive answers to their letters, and they may ensure that the letters will be shared with the class. If the write-the-author project is intended to be a more personal endeavor, students may have responses to their letters mailed to home addresses.

Writing in Care of Publishers

Some authors prefer that letters be mailed in care of their publisher(s) or agents for a variety of reasons—the need to maintain privacy, fear of retaliation for writing about controversial subjects, publishers' credit, frequent changes of address, etc. Most authors, however, seem to prefer that their mail be sent to them directly at their home addresses. Several authors have mentioned that the forwarding of mail from publishing houses is frequently delayed, even up to a year later. In defense of the publishing companies, one associate I spoke with stated that all author mail sent in care of her house was immediately forwarded. Pleasant Company, and possibly other publishers, mails correspondents who write in care of them a postcard as notification that the letter has been received and forwarded to the author. What a "pleasant" thing to do!

Occasionally, publishers are required to answer mail for very popular authors due to the overwhelming volume of mail that pours in daily. A publishing executive informed me that one of his authors receives 55,000 letters yearly and cannot possibly respond personally to them all. He added, however, that all letters are read by a staff member and letters of unique substance or great importance are forwarded to the author. Publisher responses to fan mail may take the form of a postcard, a newsletter, or a detailed personal response from a knowledgeable associate. One prolific "adult" author to whom several of my advanced readers have written does not answer his mail personally, but the personal attention given the correspondence by his staff—even the sending of informative materials—has been more than satisfactory.

"I would like mail to be sent to me c/o my publisher. At least someone there should appreciate how much mail I get and presumably how many people are reading my books. (At a publishing house they tally sales. But a single book read aloud to 24 students may result in 24 letters. I want them to know how many children are familiar with my books.)"

"I have received letters from my publisher up to one year after it was sent. If people are going to write, they may as well have the correct address!"

"I would rather have letters sent through my publishers, inconvenient as that may be, because I don't want people dropping in on me. That has happened."

"Letters to publishers often take months to reach the author."

"As you see, I prefer to have mail forwarded to me through my publishers. This is for several reasons: 1) I get brownie points from them (!) 2) I moved back to Miami to care for my elderly mother, but may not be here forever. (We'd always planned to return to North Florida.) 3) Once in a while you run across a nut who pesters you to death & I'd like to protect myself."

Should you need to write an author not listed in this volume, you may mail your letter in care of the publisher's address listed on the copyright page of the book that was read. It is preferable, if researching the address in a paperback, to use the address of the original hardback publisher rather than the distributor of the softcover. The addresses of major publishers of children's books are listed in the appendices of this volume.

Envelopes addressed to authors in care of publishers should list the author's name on the first line, the "in care of" abbreviation (c/o) followed by the name of the publishing house on the second line, the publisher's address on the third line, then the city, state, and Zip Code ® on the fourth line.

Sample: MR RANDALL JACKSON
             C/O BROOKSIDE PUBLISHING CO
             555 WASHINGTON AVE
             NEW YORK NY 10555

It is not necessary to direct the letter to a specific department within the publishing company because the divisions which handle author mail vary from house to house. Mail handling personnel at the publishing companies are familiar with the names of their authors and illustrators. They will ensure that your letter eventually reaches its final destination.

✎ Preparing for the Wait

The most difficult part of the correspondence process for both teachers and students is the agonizing wait for a response. Be prepared for the students who will ask you the day after their letters have been mailed if their answers have come. Perhaps these words from Joan Lowery Nixon will give teachers insight into the busy life of an author and help assuage the restlessness of impatient correspondents.

"Teachers don't realize that when a letter is sent to a publishing house, and from there to the author, it can take a month or two to be delivered. Even a letter sent directly to the author should allow the author at least two months to answer. Especially during March, April, and May, there are library conventions, the International Reading Association convention, young author programs, book fairs, and speaking engagements at schools, so the author is quite likely away from home for a week or two at a time. When I arrive home to face a huge stack of mail, it's the letters from family, my agent, my editors, and other business mail that takes precedence, along with galleys or page proofs to be corrected, speaking invitations to answer, and so forth. And there's always the current book to be finished with a deadline fast approaching. When I'm finally able to find time to sit down and go through the stacks of letters from students, I invariably find some dated months earlier that tell me, 'Please answer this within two weeks or I won't get a grade.' Or . . . 'My report on you is due before May first (letter dated April 15), and my teacher requires a letter from you, or I can't get an A.' "

✏️ Sharing Letters

When the letters from authors begin to filter in, it is especially nice to share the excitement with the whole class. You may want a child to read the copy of his/her letter to the author prior to sharing the response so that the letter will be more meaningful for everyone. A teacher-directed discussion after the letter sharing will further enhance the special occasion.

✏️ Follow-Up Activities

A nice follow-up to sharing author correspondence would be to present students with plastic sheet protectors to safely display their letters. Many letters may increase their worth over the years, but they will always have sentimental value for their owners. If one letter from an author is written to the whole class, the teacher should make photocopies so that each child will have something to call his own. Teachers may also photocopy all the letters from authors and illustrators to make a class scrapbook or bulletin board.

✏️ Author Visits

The ultimate follow-up to whole class correspondence with an author would be for the author to visit the children in person. Most authors are available for school visits if the price is right. Unfortunately, there are substantial expenses involved in scheduling school appearances. The honorarium may be underwritten by a grant, a donor, the local PTA, or sponsored as a school-based field trip (see Appendices).

A Message to Young Readers

Note: Though this section is written to the children, it will be most effective if it is presented orally by a teacher or librarian rather than being duplicated and distributed.

A Prerequisite of Writing Authors

Writing a letter to an author or illustrator can be a rewarding experience. Receiving an answer in the mail is even more fun. But before you write your letter, there is one important requirement you must keep in mind. **You must only write to authors or illustrators whose books you have read**. If you write an author and you are not familiar with his work, you really don't have anything to say. Ideally, you should read more than one book by an author or illustrator so you are familiar with his style and can compare his work. One good way to compare books is to read another work by the author of a book you have read together in class or your teacher or librarian has used as a read-aloud.

Valid Reasons to Write an Author

There are many fine reasons to write a letter to an author or illustrator. Some of the reasons listed here will help you form an idea of how genuine motivation to correspond with authors feels. You have good reason to write an author if:

- you are fascinated with the author's work.
- there was something in the book you didn't understand.
- you did not like the ending.
- you have read several of his/her books and can't wait for the next one.
- the book moved you to laughter or tears or provoked passionate emotions (i.e., love, happiness, rage, sadness, fear, confusion, etc.).
- you admire his/her style.
- you need advice about writing or illustrating and you respect this person's work.
- you think you found an error in the book.
- you have researched the author and still have questions.
- you are interested in the subject matter of a book and want to know more.
- you could not put the book down.
- you want to be heard because you have something valuable to say that will make a difference.

- you have an idea to share that you think would make a great story.

- you would like to share something interesting, humorous, or typical that has happened to you or your friends.

- " . . . *relevant questions, why book was chosen by reader, perceived significance of content, relate stories to their own experience, raise questions, report how the story made them feel or challenge some aspects.*"

Poor Reasons to Write an Author

There are not nearly as many poor reasons to correspond with authors as there are good reasons. However, you should not write an author if your only reason is because:

- you want a pen pal.

- it is a class assignment.

- you want to get free stuff.

- you collect autographs.

- you want to get to know the author.

- you want the author to proofread your manuscript.

- you share the same birthday.

"*I recognize the appeal of gimmicks—writing to an author whose birthday you happen to share—but I am of the opinion that the rewards are brief and ultimately misleading.*"

"*I receive countless letters from high school and university students asking me to answer pages of questions so they can write reports about me for various classes. I send them a form letter listing library sources they can easily find. Learning to do research is a valuable lesson, and—by golly—I'm too busy to do their homework for them!*" Joan Lowery Nixon

Legibility

The letter you put in the mail should be something you are proud to send. You can show how much you value what you want to say to an author or illustrator by the way your letter and envelope appear. You should always write with your neatest manuscript or cursive handwriting using a dark pencil or pen so that your letter may be clearly read and understood by the author you are writing. It is also important to write your letter using correct friendly letter format.

Letter Content

How much money do you make? Will you send me a free book? Are you married? When is your birthday? How old are you? These are some of the most commonly asked, yet most improper questions asked of authors. These questions wouldn't be asked of someone you were meeting for the first time in person, so why should they be asked in a letter? Remember, authors are people, too. Your questions should reflect upon your experience reading the author's book. Decide whether the questions you are preparing to ask are inquisitive or intrusive. But don't be afraid to be yourself. Authors enjoy hearing you tell about yourself and your interests in your own words much more than overly formal language. Be candid, use humor, and you will encourage an equally interesting response.

"It is not polite for children to address adults they have never met by their first names. (Is that how they address their teachers and principals?)"

"Tell the author something about yourself. I like to find out about my readers as much as they like to find out about me." Marilyn Singer

Return Addresses

Your teacher will let you know if you should use your home address or the school's address in your correspondence. Either way, do not forget to write your return address in the heading of your letter, in the upper left corner of your mailing envelope, and in the center of the self-addressed stamped envelope that you include with your letter.

Self-Addressed Stamped Envelopes

"Please tell your readers that the postage costs of answering a letter can exceed by many times the royalty an author earns on the sale of one copy of the book. They should always send an SASE."

Always enclose a self-addressed stamped envelope with your letter to an author or illustrator. Having readily available an envelope that is already addressed and stamped makes it easier for the author to get the response to you as quickly as possible. The author doesn't have to take time to locate and write the mailing address on the envelope, and a special trip to the post office to purchase stamps is not necessary. One $ .33 stamp is not very expensive, but do the math and you will see that $ .33 multiplied by 4 equals more than a dollar. Imagine being required to purchase 100 stamps every week—that's $33.00!

Types of Responses to Expect

"I write personal letters to the kids who sincerely tell me they want to be writers and who ask for advice. I say sincerely because I don't count the 'have to write to the author' letter in which a student writes, 'I think I want to be a writer when I grow up, except I don't want to have to learn to spell, so please answer the following questions about writing . . . ' Joan Lowery Nixon

"I do answer most of the letters I receive—a form postcard to a form letter and a real note to a real letter."

" . . . expect a group letter in response to their communication rather than individual letters."

"Many girls write two or three times wanting to be pen pals. I only wish I had the time."

"I like to get letters from anyone who's writing of his or her own free will, for her or his good reasons. I answer all such letters, sometimes at length, and there are kids I've written back-and-forth with for years."

"Children are now requesting a "personal" handwritten reply instead of a computer printed response! This makes any attempt at answering individual questions or giving advice almost impossible."

Some authors and illustrators have time or make time to write you a typed or handwritten personal letter. Others will send you a computer printed letter designed to answer your questions and either sign it or write a personal note at the bottom. Authors who receive tons of mail may only be able to send a form letter or a post card. If each child in your class is writing the same author, expect one letter from the author to the whole class. Ask your teacher to make everybody a photocopy. Try to understand and be content with the response the author is able to provide you. If you want a personal reply, make your letter so well-written and perceptive that an author must respond personally.

✎ Waiting for a Response

"If you send your letter to the author in care of the publisher, it can take quite a while before the publisher forwards your letter to the author. So, if you don't get a response right away, don't fret. Be patient." Marilyn Singer

"Patience required—I answer mail in batches." Ed Emberley

"Writers are busy people. We travel, visit schools, answer mail—and try to <u>write</u>. Sometimes I have to choose between working on a manuscript and answering kids' letters. I usually put my manuscript first and answer letters when it's on its way to New York. I really like to hear from my readers, but it may be months before I have the opportunity to reply."

"Keep it short and be prepared to wait months for an answer."

Authors and illustrators are busy people, but they are also caring people. Most authors, not only those listed in this book, will respond eventually to reader mail. Be patient.

Directory of Authors and Illustrators

Carol M. Adorjan

▲▼▲

Born: August 17, 1934
Address: 1667 Winnetka Rd.
Glenview, IL 60025

Selected Titles
1990 - I Can! Can You?
1990 - That's What Friends Are For
1990 - The Copy Cat Mystery
1988 - WKID, Easy Radio Plays
1988 - A Little Princess (adaptation)
1988 - The Big Date
1988 - The Revolt of the Eighth Grade
1987 - Eighth Grade to the Rescue
1987 - Those Crazy Eighth Grade Pictures
1981 - Pig Party
1981 - The Electric Man
1973 - The Cat Sitter Mystery
1973 - Jonathan Bloom's Room

Carol answers letters from both children and adults who have questions and comments about herself, her books, and writing in general.

A lifetime Chicago area resident, Carol Adorjan has taught high school English, history, and anthropology. Presently, she teaches writing workshops. Her first short story was published in 1956. Since then, her articles and short fiction have appeared in a variety of newspapers, trade, religious, national, and literary periodicals, here and abroad. She has had several radio plays produced, including one by the BBC. The National Radio Theatre production of *The Sea Wolf* won the 1981 Ohio State Award. Her stage plays have won competitions and have been produced in many U.S. cities. Her first children's book, *Someone I Know*, a preschool/early reader published in 1968, was revised and released in 1990 as *I Can! Can You?*

Thomas B. Allen

Illustrator

▲▼▲

Born: January 23, 1928
Address: 830 Indian Beach Dr.
Sarasota, FL 34234

Selected Titles
1998 - Good-Bye Charles Lindbergh
1997 - A Green Horn Blowing
1997 - A Place Called Freedom
1997 - Littlejim's Dreams
1996 - Poems for Youth
1995 - Across the Wide Dark Sea
1994 - Littlejim's Gift
1994 - The Days Before Now
1994 - Mountain Valor
1992 - Going West
1990 - The Random House Book of Sports Stories
1990 - Littlejim
1989 - On Grandaddy's Farm
1987 - The Secret Garden

Thomas Allen enjoys all types of correspondence from his readers.

Thomas B. Allen has taught illustration and served as head of the Department of Illustration at Ringling School of Art and Design since 1995.

Born in Tennessee, Allen began art lessons at age nine. He attended Vanderbilt University on a football scholarship, but later switched to the Art Institute of Chicago to pursue an education in fine art. In 1955, after serving as an officer in the U.S. Marine Corps, he moved to New York City where he found work as an illustrator with *Esquire* magazine.

One memorable assignment early in his career came from *Esquire* when he was sent for three weeks on location to Nevada for the film *The Misfits* with Clark Gable and Marilyn Monroe.

A professional illustrator for more than 40 years, Allen and his illustrations were featured in *Innovators of American Illustration* by Steven Heller. In the book, Heller calls Allen "a pioneer of the new impressionistic illustration."

Allen has illustrated books, magazines, record covers, and for television. His clients include *The New Yorker, Gourmet, The Atlantic, Sports Illustrated, Life, Fortune, Time,* CBS, NBC, Columbia Records, the Franklin Library, the Discovery Channel, and others.

Most of Allen's current professional work lies in the realm of children's books.

Jennifer Armstrong

Born: May 12, 1961
Address: 47 Franklin St.
          Saratoga Springs, NY 12866
E-mail: jma@aol.com

Selected Titles

1999 - In My Hands: Memories of a Holocaust Rescuer
1998 - Pockets
1998 - Shipwreck at the Bottom of the World
1997 - Sunshine, Moonshine
1997 - Mary Mehan Awake
1996 - The Snowball
1996 - Patrick Doyle Is Full of Blarney
1996 - The Dreams of Mairhe Mehan
1995 - Wan Hu Is in the Stars
1995 - Black-Eyed Susan
1994 - That Terrible Baby
1993 - Chin Yo Min and
       the Ginger Cat
1992 - Steal Away
1992 - Hugh Can Do

Jennifer Armstrong enjoys most types of correspondence from her readers, including e-mail.

Jennifer Armstrong writes:

I grew up outside of New York City in a town called South Salem. There was a North Salem, too, but no plain old Salem in between. I always wondered what happened to it.

On my desk is a picture of me when I was ten years old, sitting in front of a bookcase. It's an author photograph. I knew I was going to be an author in first grade. The other picture is my husband, James Howard Kunstler, who is also an author. It's very handy to have another writer around. He reads all my work before I send it to my editor. He's a very tough critic.

I'm at the library about three times a week. Because I write historical fiction, I spend a lot of time doing research. For *Mary Mehan Awake*, I had to research 19th-century photography, Abe Lincoln's funeral, train lines at the end of the Civil War, Niagara Falls, the rivers of Manitoba and Ontario, and a boxful of other things.

I stay inside and get a lot of work done. When it's nice out, I go outside and garden. Or read in the garden. Either one is fun. I'm not very disciplined, so winter is a good time for me to stop fooling around and pay attention. My house is old and drafty, and my office is the warmest room. You see how this would make me more productive?

I type very fast. I do all my writing on the computer. If I wrote by hand, I wouldn't be able to read it. I do have a nice signature, though, and I practice it a lot because I like autographing books. That's a lot of fun. I always sign my books on the title page right under where my name is printed. I'll never get over the thrill. Really.

Sandy Asher

Author

▲▼▲

Born: October 16, 1942
Address: c/o Drury College
         900 North Benton
         Springfield, MO 65802

Selected Titles
1996 - But That's Another Story
1993 - Out of Here: A Senior Class Yearbook
1991 - Can David Do It?
1990 - Mary-in-the-Middle
1990 - Pat's Promise
1989 - Best Friends Get Better
1989 - Princess Bee and the Royal Goodnight Story
1989 - Teddy Teabury's Peanutty Problems
1989 - Wild Words! How to Train Them to Tell Stories
1987 - Everything Is Not Enough
1987 - Where Do You Get Your Ideas? Helping Young
       Writers Begin
1985 - Teddy Teabury's Fabulous Facts
1984 - Missing Pieces
1983 - Things Are Seldom What They Seem
1982 - Just Like Jenny
1980 - Daughters of the Law
1980 - Summer Begins

With all my best wishes,
Sandy Asher

Sandy likes to hear whatever her readers want to tell or ask her. She will be happy to respond with a letter to answer questions or provide biographical and bibliographical articles, if needed.

Sandy Asher is a prolific writer of both fiction and non-fiction books and has published many articles, poems, stories, and plays. Sandy's three loves when she was growing up were dancing, acting, and writing. There came a time when she had to decide which of the three she wanted to do for the rest of her life. Writing was her choice, because she realized she would do it whether she was ever paid for it or not.

Ms. Asher explains why books are so important to young people: "A book can be the best—even the only—friend a young reader has. It's there whenever you need it, it doesn't criticize, it doesn't smother you with attention when you don't need it, and it never tells a soul which parts of it made you cry and which parts helped you to laugh. No wonder young readers are the most loyal audience any writer could ever hope to have!"

Sandy Asher is the writer-in-residence at Drury College in Springfield, Missouri, and has served as a board member for both The Assembly on Literature for Adolescents/NCTE and The Society of Children's Book Writers and Illustrators.

Jim Aylesworth

▼▲

Born: February 21, 1943
Address: 55 West Delaware Place
             Chicago, IL 60610
E-mail: oldfly@ayles.com
Web Site: www.ayles.com

Selected Titles
1999 - The Full Belly Bowl
1999 - Aunt Pitty Patty's Piggy
1998 - Through the Night
1998 - The Gingerbread Man
1997 - Teddy Bear Tears
1996 - My Sister's Rusty Bike
1996 - Wake Up, Little Children
1995 - McGraw's Emporium
1994 - My Son John
1993 - The Good-Night Kiss
1992 - The Cat and the Fiddle and More
1992 - Old Black Fly
1991 - The Folks in the Valley
1991 - Country Crossing
1990 - The Completed Hickory, Dickory, Doc
1989 - Mr. McGill Goes to Town
1989 - Mother Halverson's New Cat

Jim likes to receive letters from children or whole classes that have read his books.

When people ask Jim Aylesworth what he does for a living, he always answers that he's a teacher. And he really is, not just a teacher through his books, but a first grade teacher for more than 20 years. He asserts, "Teachers know that reading to children makes them love books, and children who love books want to learn to read, and children who want to learn in fact become better readers, and children who are better readers are more successful in school and more likely to read to their own children someday."

Using good books in the classroom gave Jim the desire to write his own books. Now that he has published more than a dozen books, he says no one is more surprised or pleased than he at his dream having come true. As Jim reads his own books to a class, he hopes that somewhere in another part of the world other teachers are reading his books to their classes. When children write and tell him that they like his books, it makes him feel very good.

"Writing children's books is my way of being the teacher beyond the walls of my classroom for children that I may never know."

Though he retired from classroom teaching in 1996, Mr. Aylesworth now visits schools full-time as an author.

Keith Baker

▲▼▲

Born: March 17, 1953
Address: 115 W. Smith St.
Seattle, WA 98119

ME

Selected Titles
1997 - Cat Tricks
1994 - Big Fat Hen
1993 - Elephants Aloft
1991 - Hide and Snake
1990 - Who Is the Beast?
1989 - The Magic Fan
1988 - The Dove's Letter

Keith Baker

Keith says he likes to receive self-initiated letters, especially those which contain blank checks!

Once a kindergarten student asked Keith Baker, "Have you been dead?"

"No," he answered. "Why did you ask me that?"

"Well," the student said, "Whenever our class talks about authors, they're dead!"

Keith would like to make it perfectly clear that he is not, nor has he ever been, dead. Had he been dead, there are many of his favorite things he would have missed—spaghetti, ice cream, *The Simpsons* (especially Lisa), *Calvin and Hobbes*, and *The Cat in the Hat*. But he would have missed his family and friends the most. He also would have missed his job, which is writing and illustrating picture books.

"My favorite part of making books is painting. I love mixing colors and smooshing paint on paper. I almost always use acrylic paint. It dries quickly, and then I can paint on top of it to fix my mistakes. Sometimes I cut and glue shapes from patterned paper onto my paintings. I have never tried gluing spaghetti onto a painting. I also like writing books. It can be hard at times, though, like when I can't think of an ending for a story. For instance, I have an idea about a turtle who swims to the bottom of the sea. He hears a voice say, 'Way down deep,' over and over again. The turtle finally gets to the bottom of the sea, but what does he find? I don't know! If you have any ideas to end this story, send them to me."

Marion Dane Bauer

▲▼▲

Born: November 20, 1938
Address: 8861 Basswood Rd.
Eden Prairie, MN 55344
E-mail: DaneBauer@aol.com

Selected Titles
1998 - Christmas in the Forest
1998 - Bear's Hiccups
1997 - If You Were Born a Kitten
1997 - Turtle Dreams
1997 - Alison's Fierce and Ugly Halloween
1997 - Alison's Puppy
1996 - Our Stories: A Fiction Workshop for
Young Authors
1996 - Alison's Wings
1995 - A Writer's Story, From Life to Fiction
1995 - When I Go Camping with Grandma
1994 - A Question of Trust
1994 - Am I Blue? Coming Out from the Silence
1992 - What's Your Story? A Young Person's
Guide to Writing Fiction
1991 - Face to Face
1986 - On My Honor

Concerning letters from her readers, Marion says, "I am delighted to know my books are being used in schools. I always love hearing from librarians and teachers, and from my readers, especially when they write because they really have something they want to say to me, not because a teacher has told them they must. Please request that students send a stamped, self-addressed, number 10 envelope with their letters."

"I was born in a small, cement milling community in Illinois and lived there until I left home for my junior year of college. I was, I suppose, a lonely child, though I never thought of myself that way."

Though Marion Dane Bauer was alone a great deal, she entertained herself by making up stories and acting them out with dolls or marbles or sticks . . . or friends when one was at hand. Many years later, she learned the skills necessary to write down the complex sagas she had created in her head. During that time, she married, taught high school and college English, and raised two children, along with a number of foster children and exchange students. Marion has been writing full-time now for over 20 years. In addition to extending her own range as an author, she is experiencing the pleasure of seeing her students publishing.

Tom Birdseye

▲▼▲

Born: July 13, 1951
Addresses: c/o Holiday House, Inc.
E-mail: birdseye@proaxis.com

Selected Titles

1997 - Under Our Skin: Kids Talk about Race
1996 - What I Believe: Kids Talk about Faith
1995 - Tarantula Shoes
1994 - She'll Be Comin' Round the Mountain
1994 - A Regular Flood of Mishap
1993 - Just Call Me Stupid
1993 - A Kid's Guide to Building Forts
1993 - Soap! Soap! Don't Forget the Soap!
1991 - Waiting for Baby
1990 - Tucker
1990 - A Song of Stars
1988 - Airmail to the Moon
1986 - I'm Going to Be Famous

Along with book-related writings and illustrations his readers send him, Tom likes to hear comments about his work.

When Tom Birdseye was a boy, writing was the last thing on his mind. Sports, crawdads, forts, secret codes, fenderless bicycles, butter pecan ice cream, and snow were way more fun. He never dreamed that he would become a published author at the age of thirty-five.

"At times it still amazes me that writing is my profession. It was such a difficult process for me when I was a kid; I can really identify with the reluctant writer in school today. Everything seemed to get in the way of my completing stories: from being left-handed, to my poor spelling skills, from punctuation woes, to especially a lack of ideas."

Fortunately for Tom, the right people came along and helped him discover the joys of writing and the truth that can be found in fiction. Though he still finds writing a challenge, Tom says, "The boy who couldn't imagine himself a writer, now can't imagine himself anything else."

Joan Blos

▲▼▲

Born: December 9, 1928
Addresses: c/o Atheneum
      c/o Morrow Junior Books
      c/o Simon & Schuster

Selected Titles
1998 - Bedtime!
1996 - Nellie Bly's Monkey: His Remarkable Story
    in His Own Words
1995 - The Hungry Little Boy
1994 - Brooklyn Doesn't Rhyme
1992 - A Seed, A Flower, A Minute, An Hour
1991 - The Heroine of the Titanic: A Tale Both True and
    Otherwise of the Life of Molly Brown
1990 - One Very Best Valentine's Day
1989 - The Grandpa Days
1987 - Old Henry
1985 - Brothers of the Heart: A Story of the Old Northwest,
    1837–1838
1980 - A Gathering of Days: A New England Girl's Journal,
    1830–1832

Joan Blos is interested in how and why a reader has selected a specific book, as well as relevant questions and comments.

When Joan Blos was a very little girl her parents wrote down the stories and poems she made up and told. Her mother was a teacher at an experimental school in New York City and Joan was enrolled there when she was about seven. In addition to academics, students had the opportunity to learn about art, music, and skills such as carpentry and type-setting (printing) in a non-sexist environment. Though she did well in English classes and continued writing in high school, Joan chose to major in physiology as a Vassar undergraduate and later earned a Master's degree in psychology. So, it was not until the mid-1960s when she and Betty Miles, an established author of children's books, collaborated on two primers that Joan began to see herself as a writer.

Looking back on those days, Joan Blos says that it was by linking writing with teaching graduate students that the field of children's literature became "a place where all I had learned about child development, all my interest in language, and all my love of books could at last come together."

Since that time, Joan Blos has written the texts of many picture books, three works of historical fiction, and two picture book biographies. And just as she had a fondness for historical fiction, so she now enjoys the research required by her books. *A Gathering of Days* was written after lengthy explorations of New England history. The book, which won the 1980 Newbery award, is now in its 20th printing.

Mary Bowman-Kruhm

Author

▲▼▲

Born: July 29
Address: 2802 Thurston Rd.
         Frederick, MD 21704
E-mail: kruhmmc@erols.com

Claudine G. Wirths

Author

▲▼▲

Born: May 9
Address: 6608 Jefferson Blvd., P.O. Box 335
         Braddock Heights, MD 21714
E-mail: claudinew@aol.com

Selected Titles

1998 - Coping with Discrimination and Prejudice
1998 - Coping with Encounters with the Police
1998 - Busy Toes
1996 - Onramp to the Internet: A Writer's Guide
       to Getting Online
1995 - UpgrAde: The High Tech Road to School
       Success
1995 - I Need to Get Along with Other Types
       of People
1994 - Choosing Is Confusing! How to Make
       Good Choices, Not Bad Guesses
1993 - Time to Be a Teen
1993 - How to Get Up When Schoolwork Gets You Down
1992 - Are You My Type? Or Why Aren't You More Like Me?
1989 - Where's My Other Sock?—How to Get Organized &
       Drive Your Parents & Teachers Crazy

"Letters from students who read our books are a delight—even when they are critical. A good letter helps us do a better job next time and it also gives us a glimpse into the life of the writer of the letter."

The writing team of Mary Bowman-Kruhm and Claudine G. Wirths has authored 21 books for children and young adults. They have also co-authored numerous articles and are contributing editors to *Children's Book Insider* newsletter. Ms. Wirths is a full-time writer and lecturer. In addition to writing and speaking, Dr. Bowman-Kruhm is a Faculty Associate at Johns Hopkins University, School of Continuing Studies. The picture book, *Busy Toes*, was written entirely online with a third author, Wendie Old, and was published under the pen name C. W. Bowie.

Jan Brett

▲▼

Born: December 1, 1949
Address: P.O. Box 5189
           Norwell, MA 02061
E-mail: janbrett@janbrett.com
Web Site: www.janbrett.com

Selected Titles

1998 - The Night Before Christmas
1997 - The Hat
1996 - Comet's Nine Lives
1995 - Armadillo Rodeo
1994 - Town Mouse
1993 - Christmas Trolls
1992 - Trouble with Trolls
1991 - Berlioz the Bear
1991 - The Owl and the Pussycat
1990 - The Wild Christmas Reindeer
1989 - The Mitten
1989 - Beauty and the Beast
1988 - The First Dog
1987 - Goldilocks and the Three Bears
1986 - The Twelve Days of Christmas
1986 - The Mother's Day Mice
1985 - Annie and the Wild Animals
1981 - Fritz and the Beautiful Horses

Jan Brett

"I love to hear from teachers and students, and look forward every day to reading the mail which arrives."

As a child, Jan Brett decided to be an illustrator and spent many hours reading and drawing. She says, "I remember the special quiet of rainy days when I felt that I could enter the pages of my beautiful picture books. Now I try to recreate that feeling of believing that the imaginary place I'm drawing really exists."

Many of Ms. Brett's ideas come from her memories as a student at the Boston Museum School where she spent hours in the Museum of Fine Arts. Travel is also a constant inspiration. Together with her husband, who is a member of the Boston Symphony Orchestra, Ms. Brett visits many of the countries of the world. She researches the architecture and costumes which appear in her work. "From cave paintings, to Norwegian sleighs, to Japanese gardens, I study the traditions of the many countries I visit, and use them as a starting point for my children's books."

Larry Dane Brimner

Born: November 5, 1949
Address: 3175 Lincoln Ave.
          San Diego, CA 92104
E-mail: ldb@cts.com
Web Site: http://home.navisoft.com/brimner

Selected Titles
1998 - Nana's Hog
1997 - How Many Ants?
1997 - Rock Climbing
1997 - Snowboarding
1995 - Merry Christmas, Old Armadillo
1990 - Cory Coleman, Grade 2
1988 - Country Bear's Good Neighbor

"Reading is the key to understanding and achievement, so I enjoy receiving mail from young people who are avid readers."

Larry Dane Brimner, born in St. Petersburg, Florida, spent his early childhood exploring Alaska's Kodiak Island. He traces his love of reading to that time in his life. Since there was no television reception and only sporadic radio reception, entertainment came in the form of books and stories. Reading and making up stories was a part of day-to-day family life. Raised in a traditional Southern family—his parents hail from Birmingham, Alabama—telling false-hoods was frowned upon but *embellishment* was encouraged. His affinity for reading led him to earn a Bachelor of Arts degree in British literature from San Diego State University, where he graduated *cum laude,* and a Master of Arts degree in writing.

During his 20-year teaching career, he began to write for publication. Larry made his debut in children's books with the publication of *BMX Freestyle* (Watts) in 1987. Readers responded by naming it an International Reading Association (IRA) Children's Choice book for 1988. Subsequent books have also proven popular with their targeted audience, having garnered nominations for several young reader awards.

David Budbill

▲▼▲

Born: June 13, 1940
Address: Box 2080
         East Hill Rd.
         Wolcott, VT 05680

Selected Titles
1978 - Bones on Black Spruce Mountain
1976 - Snowshoe Trek to Otter River
1974 - Christmas Tree Farm

Mr. Budbill prefers letters from individuals generated by their own interest.

David Budbill is a prolific poet and playwright, but he has also worked at various times in his life as a carpenter's apprentice, short order cook, manager of a coffee house, street gang worker, attendant in a mental hospital, forester, pastor, and teacher. His diverse work experience, studies in philosophy and art history, and a graduate degree in theology provide him an extensive idea bank for writing. David published three children's titles in the 1970s. After a hiatus of 14 years, he has returned to young adult fiction and is working on a novel entitled *Samovar and Zeemahoola.*

In response to an inquiry concerning challenges to his book *Bones on Black Spruce Mountain,* David replied, "*Bones* obviously is only 'too' mature for the school board, not for the kids. No, I don't think they will ever catch on."

Mr. Budbill has two new young adult books in the works.

Betsy Byars

▲▼▲

Born: August 7, 1928
Address: 126 Riverpoint Dr.
Clemson, SC 29631

Selected Titles
1996 - Tornado
1994 - The Dark Stairs (a Herculeah Jones
mystery)
1993 - McMummy
1992 - Coast to Coast
1991 - Wanted . . . Mud Blossom
1990 - Hooray for the Golly Sisters
1989 - Bingo Brown and the Language of Love
1986 - The Not-Just-Anybody Family
1985 - Cracker Jackson
1980 - The Night Swimmers
1977 - The Pinballs
1973 - The 18th Emergency
1970 - The Summer of the Swans
1969 - Trouble River
1968 - The Midnight Fox

Betsy likes to hear from any reader who has enjoyed one of her books.

Betsy Byars began freelance writing for magazines in the 1950s while she was a young mother, and published her first book, *Clementine*, in 1962. Since then she has published over 50 books. Her books have been translated into nine languages and several have been made into television movies. *The Summer of the Swans*, a book about a teenage girl whose mentally challenged brother runs away from home, won the Newbery Medal in 1971. Two of Betsy's children, Laurie Myers and Betsy Duffey, have followed in their mother's footsteps to become published authors themselves.

Betsy doesn't agree with the belief that you should write what you know. She says, "You've got to make up stuff!"

Betsy now lives on an airstrip in South Carolina. The bottom floor of the house is a hangar so she and her husband can just taxi out and take off.

Ann Cameron

Author

▲▼▲

Born: October 21, 1943
Address: Calle Principal
　　　　　Panajachel, Solalá
　　　　　Guatemala
　　　　　Central America
E-mail: anncameron@guate.net

Selected Titles
1998 - The Secret Life of Amanda K. Woods
1997 - More Stories Huey Tells
1995 - The Stories Huey Tells
1990 - Julian, Dream Doctor
1990 - The Kidnapped Prince: The Life of Olaudah
　　　　　Equiano (adaptation)
1988 - The Most Beautiful Place in the World
1988 - Julian, Secret Agent
1987 - Julian's Glorious Summer
1986 - More Stories Julian Tells
1981 - The Stories Julian Tells

Ann Cameron

Ann Cameron says, "I always wanted to write stories that would include the emotions all children feel. Now that I've heard from children around the world who like my books I'm delighted to find that I've really done it. I'd really like to know about kids' problems and funny things that have happened to them."

Ann Cameron was born in Rice Lake, Wisconsin, in 1943 in the middle of a blizzard. She grew up on the outskirts of that small town exploring nature—picking wild violets, staring into the eyes of cows and horses, puzzling over where the sun went at sunset, and wanting to follow it. She says, "When I was a child I fell in love with nature, imagination, and freedom. Later my childhood friends and I made up our own games. We spent lots of time outside, skiing, hiking, biking, and fishing. Our world seemed to us almost separate from the world of adults. I think the independence my childhood friends and I enjoyed is disappearing from the life of many American children, and I want them to feel it through my books."

Ann received a Bachelor of Arts degree from Harvard University in 1965 and a Master of Fine Arts degree from the University of Iowa in 1972. She lived in New York City for many years before moving to Guatemala because, she says, she wanted to experience the way of life of another culture. In Guatemala she has worked to improve the Panajachel library so that Guatemalan children will have the same opportunities to read, learn, and dream that American children enjoy. She is married to Bill Cherry, a retired staff director of a subcommittee of the U.S. House of Representatives. They live in view of three volcanoes, a beautiful lake, and a waterfall, in a small house with flowers growing over the roof and a lemon tree in the garden.

Angelica Shirley Carpenter

▲▼▲

Born: March 28, 1945
Address: c/o Palm Springs Library
         217 Cypress Ln.
         Palm Springs, FL 33461
E-mail: angelica@pbfreenet.seflin.org

Selected Titles

1997 - Robert Louis Stevenson: Finding Treasure
       Island
1992 - L. Frank Baum: Royal Historian of Oz
1990 - Frances Hodgson Burnett: Beyond the
       Secret Garden

Angelica enjoys hearing from people who have read her books and is especially interested in what motivates them to write to her.

Angelica Shirley Carpenter is the co-author of three illustrated biographies for young people. She is writing on her own now since the death of her mother and co-author, Jean Shirley, in 1995.

"Mother inspired me," says Angelica. "Writing gave us something fun to do together." Angelica has a bachelor's degree in French and master's degrees in education and library science. She began writing book reviews for a local newspaper in the late 1970s, with some being nationally syndicated. This led to many other writing opportunities including short stories, articles, and television scripts.

Since 1982, she has been director of the public library in Palm Springs, Florida. As president of the Palm Beach County Library Association, she founded BookFest, a literary festival, in 1991, and currently serves on the BookFest Board of Directors.

An accomplished photographer, Angelica produces slide-illustrated travelogues to accompany her books and is a sought-after speaker for all ages. She belongs to the Robert Louis Stevenson Club and is a member of the conference planning committee for the International Wizard of Oz Club.

Barbara Casey

Author

Born: July 11
Address: 2158 Portland Ave.
            Wellington, FL 33414
E-mail: BARCAFER@aol.com

Selected Titles
1995 - Grandma Jock and Christabelle
1992 - Leilani Zan

Barbara Casey enjoys all types of mail from her readers.

Originally from Carrollton, Illinois, Barbara Casey has been writing full-time since 1990. Her award-winning articles, short stories, and poetry for adults have appeared in several publications including the *American Poetry Anthology,* the *Sparrowgrass Poetry Forum,* the *North Carolina Christian Advocate Magazine, The New East Magazine,* the Raleigh (N.C.) *News and Observer,* and the Rocky Mount (N.C.) *Sunday Telegram.* A 30-minute television special which Ms. Casey wrote and coordinated was broadcast on WRAL, Channel 5, in Raleigh, North Carolina.

Ms. Casey's award-winning, science fiction short story for adults was featured in *The Cosmic Unicorn,* a short story anthology. Her essays, also written for adults, appear in *The Chrysalis Reader,* the national literary journal of the Swedenborg Foundation.

Ms. Casey has been a guest author and panelist at BookFest of Palm Beach, Florida, and serves as judge for the Pathfinder Literary Awards in Palm Beach and Martin Counties, Florida. She is the publisher of *Publishers Update,* a bimonthly directory of publishers, and is the Florida Regional Advisor for the Society of Children's Book Writers and Illustrators.

Peter Catalanotto

Author/ Illustrator

▲▼

Born: March 21, 1959
Address: c/o Orchard Books

Selected Titles
1998 - Letter to the Lake
1996 - My House Has Stars
1995 - The Painter
1993 - Dreamplace
1992 - Who Came Down That Road?
1992 - An Angel for Solomon Singer
1991 - Christmas Always . . .
1991 - Cecil's Story
1990 - Mr. Mumble
1989 - Dylan's Day Out
1988 - All I See

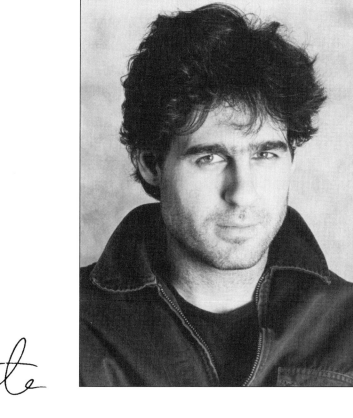

Peter likes to hear comments and questions about specific books in the letters he receives from his readers.

When Peter Catalanotto was in kindergarten, his teacher asked him if he wanted to be an artist when he grew up. He looked at her slightly confused and answered, "I'm an artist now." At the age of 13, he knew he wanted to paint and illustrate professionally, though at the time he had not associated illustrators with all those books in the library. After college, he started painting for *Reader's Digest, Family Circle,* and *Woman's Day.* Eventually, he was illustrating more than 20 book covers a year. After he did the cover for Judy Blume's *Just as Long as We're Together* in 1987, the editor offered him his first picture book manuscript, *All I See* by Cynthia Rylant. The next year, he wrote and illustrated his own picture book, *Dylan's Day Out.* Peter usually has no contact with the writers of other books he illustrates. "I'm supposed to be influenced by what the writer has created, not by the writer. It's not my job to interpret the writing, but to extend the story."

Peter's studio is in the top part of his house, and his favorite medium is watercolor because he likes its versatility. He often gets his ideas from asking himself, "What if . . . ?"

Eth Clifford

▲▼▲

Born: December 25, 1915
Address: 1075 N.E. Miami Gardens Dr. #102W
          North Miami Beach, FL 33179

Selected Titles
1998 - Ghost School
1997 - Flatfoot Fox and the Case of the Missing
       Schoolhouse
1995 - Flatfoot Fox and the Case of the Bashful Beaver
1993 - Flatfoot Fox and the Case of the Missing
       Whooooo
1993 - Never Hit a Ghost with a Baseball Bat
1992 - The Summer of the Dancing Horse
1992 - Will Somebody Please Marry My Sister?
1991 - Flatfoot Fox and the Case of the Nosy Otter
1990 - Flatfoot Fox and the Case of the Missing Eye
1990 - Harvey's Wacky Parrot Adventure
1989 - I Hate Your Guts, Ben Brooster
1988 - Scared Silly
1987 - The Man Who Sang in the Dark
1987 - Harvey's Marvelous Monkey Mystery
1986 - I Never Wanted to Be Famous
1985 - The Remembering Box
1984 - The Strange Reincarnations of Hendrik Verloom
1983 - Just Tell Me When We're Dead
1979 - Help! I'm a Prisoner in the Library

Eth Clifford

Eth Clifford responds to questions and comments about specific books or writing in general.

Eth Clifford has published over 83 books for children and adults and won many awards for her writing. Like most authors, she believes that reading lots of good literature provides the foundation for good writing, and writing a lot helps also. Eth advises, "Write letters, essays, diary entries—anything!"

Interestingly enough, Eth believes that letter writing is responsible for her being an author today. Her husband served in the South Pacific during World War II, so she filled her lonely hours writing letters to him. With his encouragement, she wrote her first novel. Real-life incidents that emerge from her roles of wife, mother, and grandmother provide Eth ideas for her books. Eth Clifford's golden rule for writing a story is—Know Your Ending!

Sneed B. Collard, III

▲▽

Born: November 7, 1959

Address: c/o Charlesbridge Publishing
c/o Houghton Mifflin Children's Books

Web Site: http://www.author-illustr-source.com/
ais_5mt.htm

Selected Titles

2000 - Making Animal Babies
1999 - One Thousand Years Ago on Planet Earth
1999 - Birds of Prey
1999 - Forest in the Clouds
1998 - Animal Dazzlers
1998 - Our Wet World: Discovering Earth's Aquatic
Ecosystems
1997 - Creepy Creatures
1997 - Monteverde: Science and Scientists in a Costa Rican
Cloud Forest
1997 - Animal Dads
1996 - Alien Invaders: The Continuing Threat
of Exotic Species
1996 - Our Natural Homes, Exploring the
Terrestrial Biomes of
North and South America
1993 - Sea Snakes

"From students, I enjoy reading letters about what they found interesting in my books and telling me stories about special animals they've encountered. From teachers, I like hearing how they've used my books in the classroom. Any good cookie recipes are also appreciated."

Since 1983, Sneed B. Collard, III, has been a biologist, computer scientist, author, and speaker. He began writing after graduating with honors in marine biology from the University of California at Berkeley. After earning his Master's in scientific instrumentation at U. C. Santa Barbara, he continued to hone his craft while serving as a computer consultant for biologists.

The main focus of Sneed's work has always been nature, science, and the environment. In his work, Sneed seeks not only to educate, entertain, and inspire children, but to empower them to effect positive change. In addition to his writing activities, he is an active speaker. He has won numerous speaking awards and addresses thousands of students and educators each year about writing and science.

Currently, Sneed resides in Missoula, Montana. When he is not writing or speaking, he enjoys hiking, going to movies, playing volleyball, cross-country skiing, and listening to rock and roll music.

Christopher Collier

▲▼▲

Born: January 29, 1930
Address: 344 West River Rd.
Orange, CT 06477

Selected Titles
1994 - With Every Drop of Blood
1992 - The Clock
1984 - Who Is Carrie?
1983 - War Comes to Willy Freeman
1981 - Jump Ship to Freedom
1978 - The Winter Hero
1976 - The Bloody Country
1974 - My Brother Sam Is Dead

Mr. Collier prefers brief letters from children who have comments about specific books.

Along with his brother, James Lincoln Collier, Christopher Collier has written many historical novels. Christopher conducts the research behind the books, while James specializes in words on the page. The events that occur in the books written by the Collier brothers actually happened to real people who lived during the historical periods which provide the books' settings. The Colliers' most renowned book, *My Brother Sam Is Dead*, was a Newbery Honor Book, a National Book Award nominee, and a Jane Addams Peace Prize Honor Book. The Collier brothers have written a 15-volume narrative history of the United States collectively titled *The Drama of American History* (Marshall/Cavendish, 1998). Christopher is a professor of history at the University of Connecticut specializing in early American history. Most of his writing is scholarship aimed at an academic readership.

Caroline B. Cooney

▲▼▲

Born: May 10, 1947
Address: P.O. Box 978
Westbrook, CT 06498

Selected Titles
1997 - What Child Is This?
1997 - The Voice on the Radio
1997 - Wanted!
1997 - The Terrorist
1996 - Flash Fire
1996 - Out of Time
1995 - Both Sides of Time
1995 - Driver's Ed
1993 - Whatever Happened to Janie?
1992 - The Return of the Vampire
1992 - Flight 116 Is Down
1992 - The Perfume
1991 - The Cheerleader
1990 - The Face on the Milk Carton

Caroline likes receiving all types of correspondence from librarians, teachers, and children and she adds, "I enjoy reading what the children have to tell me about themselves."

Caroline B. Cooney knew she wanted to be a writer when she was in sixth grade. The best teacher she ever had in her life inspired her that year by making writing his main focus. Caroline started writing then and never stopped. By the time she was a freshman in college, she was working on her first book. She wrote eight novels for adults, but none of them were ever published. While her children were young, Ms. Cooney tried writing for young people and began selling stories to *Seventeen* magazine. Later, an editor asked her if she'd ever written a book. Everything seemed to fall in place. Now, she has written over 60 books for young adults, in virtually every genre, including, humor, romance, and horror. Caroline says suspense is her favorite genre to write because action and adventure will really hold a kid's attention. Her favorite fan letter came from a girl whose grandmother forced her to read one of Caroline's books she had given her for Christmas. Though the child had been a reluctant reader, she went on to tell Caroline that she had come to an important decision—to read a second book.

Lynn Cullen

Author

Born: July 11, 1955
Address: 1839 Alderbrook Rd.
Atlanta, GA 30345

Selected Title
1998 - The Mightiest Heart
1998 - Stink Bomb
1997 - Regina Calhoun Eats Dog Food
1996 - The Three Lives of Harris Harper
1993 - The Backyard Ghost

Lynn enjoys receiving all types of correspondence from students, teachers, and librarians.

Lynn Cullen grew up in Fort Wayne, Indiana, and graduated from Indiana University. She now lives in Atlanta, Georgia, with her husband, three daughters, a Labrador Retriever named Yogi, and two cats. By reading the historical markers that dot the streets in her neighborhood, she found that Civil War soldiers may have marched through her backyard, thus sparking the idea for her first book, *The Backyard Ghost*.

Lynn Cullen says: "One of the things I like best about being an author of children's books is speaking to groups of kids about writing. I want them to know that anyone who loves to write and is willing to learn can be an author. You just have to perservere, be willing to push your limits, and most importantly, believe in yourself."

Debbie Dadey

▲▽▲

Born: May 18, 1959
Address: c/o Scholastic, Inc.
Web Site: baileykids.com

Selected Titles
2000 - Cherokee Sister
1999 - Will Rogers
1999 - King of the Kooties
1998 - Bobby and the Big Blue Bulldog
1998 - Bobby and the Stinky Brown Shoes
1997 - Shooting Star
1997 - Marty the Mudwrestler
1997 - Marty the Millionaire
1997 - Bobby and the Great Green Booger
1996 - My Mom The Frog
1996 - Marty the Maniac
1994 - Buffalo Bill and the Pony Express
Series
The Adventures of the Bailey School Kids
The Bailey City Monsters
Triplet Trouble

Debbie Dadey says "I enjoy all kinds of mail. It certainly warms my heart when I receive letters telling me that I never liked reading until I read one of your books!"

Debbie Dadey is the co-author of a best-selling series for Scholastic, Inc. *The Bailey School Kids* has been so successful Scholastic asked Debbie and her co-author, Marcia Thornton Jones, to develop an easier series for second graders, called *Triplet Trouble*. The Scholastic series, *Bailey City Monsters,* has also been released. Debbie and Marcia are currently hard at work on a book on writing for children to be published by Writers Digest.

Debbie lives in Aurora, Illinois, with her husband, Eric. They have two children, Nathan and Rebekah. Debbie is a former teacher and librarian from Kentucky, where her Scholastic co-author still lives. The two write via the fax, e-mail, and phone.

Frederick Drimmer

▲▼▲

Born: August 8, 1916
Address: c/o Atheneum

Selected Titles
1997 - Incredible People: Five Stories of Extraordinary
       Lives
1992 - Body Snatchers, Stiffs and Other Ghoulish
       Delights
1991 - Very Special People: The Struggles,
       Loves and Triumphs of Human Oddities
1991 - Born Different: Amazing Stories of Some Very
       Special People
1990 - Until You Are Dead: The Book of Executions in
       America
1985 - Captured by the Indians: Fifteen Firsthand
       Accounts, 1750-1870
1985 - The Elephant Man

Frederick Drimmer

Mr. Drimmer prefers to correspond with teachers, librarians, or whole classes.

When Frederick Drimmer was a child, he wrote a poem about the benefits of saving for a savings bank. He was rewarded with his name gold-embossed on a pencil and with seeing the poem in print.

"The praise I received convinced me this was the way to go," he says. Frederick continued writing throughout high school and college, then he got his first job as an editor for a book publisher. Mr. Drimmer has written several assigned books for publishers, but the ones that mean the most to him are the ones that have sprung from his own interests. Though they may seem scary to some, Mr. Drimmer's books about human oddities, cadavers, executions, and kidnappings have been extremely popular with young readers. Mr. Drimmer handles the difficult subjects with sensitivity and respect.

"My aim was to show, first, that even people with severe birth defects, who may look very different from the rest of us, have exactly the same feelings as anybody else, and should be treated not as curiosities but as fellow human beings. Secondly, my aim was to show how the people in my book, although burdened with great handicaps, managed to overcome them or compensate for them so well that they won the respect and admiration of everyone who saw them."

The New York Public Library named Mr. Drimmer's *Incredible People* one of the best books of the year for teenage readers.

Arlene Dubanevich

▲▼

Born: December 6, 1950
Address: 59 South Rd.
Portland, CT 06480

Selected Titles
1993 - Calico Cows
1990 - Tom's Tail
1989 - The Piggest Show on Earth
1986 - Pigs At Christmas
1985 - Pig William
1983 - Pigs in Hiding
1981 - Hearts

A. Dubanevich
PIGS IN HIDING
PIG WILLIAM
TOM'S TAIL
CALICO COWS

Ms. Dubanevich likes to correspond with writers of short letters or postcards.

Arlene Dubanevich worked as a freelance illustrator for ten years before her first children's picture book, *Pigs in Hiding*, was published. *Pigs in Hiding* won the Parent's Choice Award for illustration. The book was also published in Denmark, France, the Netherlands, and several other countries. Arlene has gone on to use her talent to write and illustrate books that include plenty of humorous dialogue not only for pigs, but for cats, mice, cows, and big chickens! She lives with her husband, dog, and bird in a barn in the woods of central Connecticut and takes time out from writing to tend her flower gardens, cook Mexican food, and play racquetball.

Ed Emberley

▲▽▲

Born: October 19, 1931
Address: 6 Water St.
　　　　　　Ipswich, MA 01938

Selected Titles

1998 - Three: An Emberley Family Scrapbook
1997 - Glad Monster, Sad Monster: A Book about Feelings
1993 - Go Away, Big Green Monster!
1992 - Ed Emberley's Thumbprint Drawing Box
1991 - Space City
1990 - Picture Pie: A Drawing Book
1990 - Little Drawing Book of Horses
1990 - Little Drawing Book of Trucks
1988 - Ed Emberley's Drawing Box
1987 - Christmas Drawing Book
1987 - The Moon Seems to Change
1985 - Meet the Computer
1967 - Drummer Hoff
1967 - Ladybug, Ladybug, Fly Away Home
1966 - One Wide River to Cross
1965 - Punch and Judy: A Play for Puppets
1961 - The Wing on a Flea: A Book about Shapes

"Patience required—I answer mail in batches."

Ed Emberley, winner of the 1968 Caldecott Medal for his book *Drummer Hoff,* disagrees with many of the "authorities" whose "research proves" that copying and imitating art are detrimental to the creativity of a child.

"I realize that being a children's book illustrator doesn't give me credentials to speak with authority about the art education of young children. (I'm not, after all, an expert in education . . . nor children . . . nor, for that matter, art.) But it does give me a platform and while I have it I'm going to use it." Mr. Emberley believes that copying can be both a source of information and inspiration. "The fact is, some of the artists whose work we most admire today copied to learn."

Mr. Emberley has been writing and illustrating children's literature for over 30 years. In the past, he has used a variety of media in his artwork such as pencil, pen-and-ink, and woodcuts. Now, he uses a computer to make all of his drawings, from sketches to final art. Not the only creative mind in his family, Ed's wife Barbara, his son Michael, and daughter Rebecca are also authors and illustrators of children's books.

Tom Feelings

▲▼▲

Born: May 19, 1933
Address: 180 Wateree Ave.
Columbia, SC 29205

Selected Titles
1995 - The Middle Passage: White Ships, Black Cargo
1993 - Soul Looks Back in Wonder
1992 - Talking with Artists (contributor)
1991 - Tommy Traveler in the World of Black History
1987 - Now Sheba Sings the Song
1981 - Black Child
1981 - Daydreamers
1978 - Something on My Mind
1976 - From Slave to Abolitionist: The Life of William
         Wells Brown
1974 - Jambo Means Hello
1971 - Moja Means One
1970 - Black Folktales
1970 - Zamani Goes to Market
1968 - To Be a Slave
1968 - The Congo, River of Mystery
1967 - Bola and the Oba's Drummers

Mr. Feelings enjoys hearing comments about specific books he has written or illustrated.

Tom Feelings began drawing when he was four or five years old and started telling stories with pictures at the age of nine. As an adult he attended art school, served in the air force, and worked as a teacher and consultant in both Africa and South America. In 1969, *To Be a Slave*, written by Julius Lester and illustrated by Tom Feelings, was selected as a Newbery Honor Book. Later, two of Tom's books, *Moja Means One* and *Jambo Means Hello* were named Caldecott Honor Books. His most recent work depicts the journeys of slaves from Africa to America. Tom began creating the 50 plus black and white paintings for his adult picture book, *The Middle Passage*, in 1974—20 years prior to its publication.

Tom says, "I'm like an old Southern black preacher or a choir singing out to you, reaching out—you have to respond."

Leonard Everett Fisher

Born: June 24, 1924
Address: 7 Twin Bridge Acre Rd.
　　　　　Westport, CT 06880
E-mail: LeonardoE1@aol.com
Web Site: www.bergenstein.com/SCBWI/fisher/
　　　　　fisher.htm

Selected Titles

1998 - To Bigotry No Sanction
1997 - The Jetty Chronicles
1997 - Anasazi
1997 - God and Goddesses of Ancient Egypt
1996 - William Tell
1995 - Gandhi
1994 - Kinderdike
1993 - Gutenberg
1992 - Tracks across America: The Story of the
　　　　American Railroad, 1825-1900
1992 - Galileo
1990 - The Oregon Trail
1989 - The Wailing Wall
1988 - Pyramid of the Sun • Pyramid of the Moon
1987 - The Alamo
1986 - The Great Wall of China
1984 - The Olympians: Great Gods and Goddesses of Ancient Greece

Comments and questions about books, writing, and illustrating interest Mr. Fisher.

When Leonard Everett Fisher was two, he painted over an illustration done by his father, who had always dreamed of becoming an artist. Instead of being punished, he was rewarded with a table and art supplies. "I performed a single compulsive act that led to all that I am and ever will be. Perhaps it was not compulsion at all, but a predestined beginning."

Today Mr. Fisher has illustrated more than 200 books, over 60 of which he also authored. Prior to his publishing career, he served as a map maker in the army during World War II, earned two art degrees from Yale, and won the Pulitzer Prize for painting. He has also designed ten United States postage stamps.

"I am a picture maker—painter, illustrator, and writer. Paints, inks, pens, leads, typewriters, and words are the instruments of my expression. I create books—not books for young people or books for old people—just books." says Leonard Everett Fisher.

Ina R. Friedman

Born: January 6, 1926
Address: 311 Dean Rd.
         Brookline, MA 02146
E-mail: starobin@tiac.net
Web Site: www.tiac.net/users/starobin/

Selected Titles

1997 - Black Cop: The Biography of Tilmon B.
       O'Bryant
1995 - Flying against the Wind: The Story of a Young
       Woman Who Defied the Nazis
1990 - The Other Victims: First-Person Stories of Non-
       Jews Persecuted by the Nazis
1984 - How My Parents Learned to Eat
1982 - Escape or Die: True Stories of Young People
       Who Survived the Holocaust

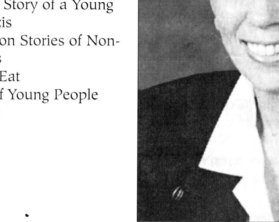

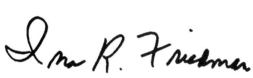

Letters which contain comments and questions about specific books interest Ms. Friedman.

An author and storyteller, Ina R. Friedman's three biographies on World War II present a trilogy on Christians and Jewish teenagers growing up in a totalitarian regime. *Escape or Die* portrays the courage and ingenuity of Jewish teenagers who survived against all odds. *The Other Victims* tells the personal stories of non-Jews, such as Gypsies, Jehovah's Witnesses, homosexuals, the handicapped and political opponents of the Nazis who escaped being among the five million non-Jews deliberately murdered by the Third Reich for political and racial reasons. *Flying against the Wind* is the rare story of one of the few non-Jewish Germans to resist the Nazis. An "Aryan," the heroine resisted peer pressure and Nazi propaganda to help Hitler's victims. Ms. Friedman's extensive research (she traveled over 70,000 miles to collect these interviews) and a graduate degree in storytelling make her highly qualified for public speaking engagements. Through the drama of storytelling, she helps young people reduce overwhelming numbers to the effects of the Holocaust on individuals like themselves.

Jean Fritz

Born: November 16, 1915
Address: 50 Bellewood Ave.
Dobbs Ferry, NY 10522

Selected Titles

1995 - You Want Women to Vote, Lizzie Stanton?
1994 - Harriet Beecher Stowe and the Beecher
Preachers
1993 - Surprising Myself
1993 - Around the World in a Hundred Years:
Henry the Navigator
1993 - Just a Few Words, Mr. Lincoln: The Story of
the Gettysburg Address
1992 - The World in 1492 (editor & contributor)
1991 - Bully for You, Teddy Roosevelt!
1987 - Shh! We're Writing the Constitution
1985 - China Homecoming
1983 - The Double Life of Pocahontas
1982 - Homesick: My Own Story
1981 - Traitor: The Case of Benedict Arnold
1981 - The Man Who Loved Books
1976 - Will You Sign Here, John Hancock?
1975 - Who's That Stepping on Plymouth Rock?
1960 - Brady
1958 - The Cabin Faced West

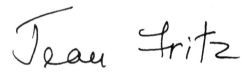

Jean Fritz is interested in what the child wants to know.

When people ask Jean Fritz how she picks the subjects for her biographies, she responds, "Actually, I don't feel that I do pick them. They seem to pick me. Suddenly there they are, speaking to me." While researching a historical figure she tries to find something strange or unique that will help her and her readers understand the character better. "Sometimes I become impatient with the myths that have sprung up around history. When I can, I try to set the record straight."

Rather than use a word processor, Ms. Fritz writes all of her books by hand and revises daily by reading everything she has written up to that point. Born in China, the child of missionaries, Jean enjoys traveling, especially to places where the people she writes about lived, "wild places," and the ocean. In response to the homesickness she felt as a child, Jean says, "No one is more patriotic than the one separated from his or her country. No one is as eager to find roots as the person who has been uprooted."

Jack Gantos

▲▼

Born: July 2, 1951
Address: 1666 Cerro Gordo Rd.
Santa Fe, NM 87501

Selected Titles
1999 - Jack on the Tracks
1998 - Back to School for Rotten Ralph
1998 - Joey Pigza Swallowed the Key
1997 - Jack's Black Book
1997 - Desire Lines
1996 - Jack's New Power
1994 - Heads or Tails (Stories from My Sixth Grade Diaries)
1994 - Not So Rotten Ralph
1990 - Happy Birthday Rotten Ralph
1989 - Rotten Ralph's Show and Tell
1986 - Rotten Ralph's Trick or Treat
1984 - Rotten Ralph's Rotten Christmas
1982 - Worse Than Rotten Ralph
1976 - Rotten Ralph

Jack Gantos likes to hear details from his readers' lives as young writers.

When Jack Gantos was in second grade he got his first diary. His mother said he was too young, but because he so wanted to copy his older sister he threw a temper tantrum and got what he wanted. "I wrote in my diary every day. I wrote the date, the weather and what I ate for breakfast, lunch, and dinner. Food was the most important thing in the world to me, and so I wrote about it all the time."

Jack continued to keep journals all through junior high and high school, writing about personal experiences—a plane crash he witnessed, his father's heroic rescue efforts, and the burning of his family's home. Knowing he wanted to pursue a career that would be both challenging and rewarding, he enrolled in Emerson College to study creative writing and literature. While in college, Jack teamed up with Nicole Rubel, a painting student at the Museum School of Fine Arts, and they began working together on picture books. Many of their projects were rejected, but their hard work paid off with the publication of *Rotten Ralph*, an idea generated by Jack's rogue pet cat.

Mr. Gantos says, "I still read and write in my journal each day. I continue to write many kinds of books and use my personal experiences for inspiration."

Sherry Garland

Author

Born: July 24, 1948
Address: c/o Harcourt Brace
E-mail: Garlanslg@aol.com

Selected Titles

2000 - Dragon Tales: Selected Stories from Vietnam
1999 - Journey of the Eagle
1999 - Goodnight Cowboy
1999 - Voices of the Alamo
1998 - Writing for Young Adults
1998 - A Line in the Sand: The Alamo Diary of
Lucinda Lawrence
1998 - My Father's Boat
1997 - The Last Rainmaker
1996 - Letters from the Mountain
1995 - Cabin 102
1995 - The Summer Sands
1995 - Indio
1994 - I Never Knew Your Name
1993 - Shadow of the Dragon
1993 - The Silent Storm
1993 - The Lotus Seed
1992 - Song of the Buffalo Boy
1990 - Vietnam: Rebuilding a Nation

Ms. Garland enjoys receiving all types of letters from children.

The youngest of nine children, Sherry Garland grew up on farms and in small towns in Texas. Her family was too poor to buy many books, so she created her own stories while exploring the woods and meadows. Ms. Garland's writing career began in high school when she won an essay writing contest. "My essay was printed in the newspaper, I appeared on TV, and was honored at a banquet where I received $100. All that fame and glory convinced me that writing would be an exciting career."

Sherry wrote two adult books before switching to writing for younger readers. Several of her award-winning books focus on Vietnam and evolved from her close association with Vietnamese families in Houston, Texas. She has traveled across the USA and to Asia, speaking at schools and conferences about writing children's books. Concerning corresponding with readers, Sherry says, "Receiving fan mail is one of the biggest rewards of being an author. It helps me to keep in touch with the feelings of readers."

Gail Gibbons

▲▼▲

Born: August 1, 1944
Address: Goose Green
           Corinth, VT 05039
Web Site: www.gailgibbons.com

Selected Titles
1998 - Soaring with the Wind/Bald Eagles
1998 - Yippee-Yay! A Book about Cowboys and Cowgirls
1998 - Marshes and Swamps
1998 - Penguins
1998 - The Art Box
1997 - Click! A Book about Cameras and
       Taking Pictures
1997 - The Honey Makers
1997 - Gulls . . . Gulls . . . Gulls
1997 - The Moon Book
1996 - Knights in Shining Armor
1996 - Cats
1996 - Dogs
1996 - Deserts
1994 - Wolves
1994 - Emergency
1994 - Nature's Green Umbrella: Tropical Rain Forests
1993 - The Planets
1993 - Spiders

Gail Gibbons enjoys responding to questions posed by her young readers.

ALA *Booklist* calls Gail Gibbons "a master of picture book nonfiction." Gail explains, "To me, putting a nonfiction book together is like watching the pieces of a puzzle finally fitting together." Both an author and illustrator, Ms. Gibbons enjoys researching her books and answering the self-imposed question, "How does it work?"

When Gail was a child growing up in Illinois, she began writing stories, drawing pictures for them, and binding the pages together with yarn to make her own books. Later, she graduated from the University of Illinois with a Bachelor of Fine Art in graphic design and began working as a television artist. After working at NBC in New York on *The Today Show, Saturday Night Live*, and the children's show *Take a Giant Step*, she returned full-time to her first love—writing and illustrating children's books.

Gail's favorite letter from a child goes like this: "Dear Gail, I love your books. Right now I am—oh there's a spider crawling across the page! SQUASH." Gail recalls, "There was a dead spider squashed right on the letter. It was hysterical. I saved that letter. And I still have the dead spider!"

James Cross Giblin

▲▼

Born: July 8, 1933
Address: 200 East 24th St. Apt. 1606
New York, NY 10010

Selected Titles
1997 - Charles A. Lindbergh: A Human Hero
1996 - The Dwarf, the Giant, and the Unicorn: A Tale
of King Arthur
1995 - When Plague Strikes: The Black Death,
Smallpox, AIDS
1994 - Thomas Jefferson: A Picture Book Biography
1993 - Be Seated: A Book about Chairs
1992 - George Washington: A Picture Book Biography
1991 - The Truth about Unicorns
1990 - Writing Books for Young People
1990 - The Riddle of the Rosetta Stone: Key to Ancient
Egypt
1987 - From Hand to Mouth: Or How We Invented
Knives, Forks, Spoons, & Chopsticks, & the
Table Manners to Go with Them
1986 - Milk: The Fight for Purity
1985 - The Truth about Santa Claus
1983 - Fireworks, Picnics, & Flags:
The Story of the Fourth of July Symbols
1982 - Chimney Sweeps: Yesterday & Today

Questions and comments from his readers of all ages interest Mr. Giblin.

"In writing nonfiction, as with other types of books, I believe it's absolutely essential for the author to be enthusiastic about his or her topic. Only then can one hope to generate enthusiasm in readers."

James Cross Giblin is both an author and editor of children's books. He fell in love with literature as a child growing up in a house full of books. In addition to making up stories as a boy, James wrote feature articles for his school newspapers in both junior high and high school. While attending Case Western Reserve University in Cleveland, Ohio, he even tried his hand as a playwright. "I've learned so much and had so much fun while researching my children's books. I only hope my pleasure communicates itself to young readers and makes them want to read more books. If it does," Mr. Giblin shares, "I'll be repaying the debt I owe all the fine writers who nurtured my love of reading when I was a child."

Mr. Giblin's work in progress is *The Mystery of the Mammoth Bones, and How It Was Solved.*

Sue Goldberg

▲▼

Born: January 1, 1948
Address: c/o Simon & Schuster, Inc.

  c/o Friends of the Zoo
  International Wildlife Conservation
  Park
  Bronx Zoo
  Bronx, NY 10460

Selected Title
1991 - Dear Bronx Zoo

Sue Goldberg enjoys hearing about readers' experiences with animals and she will respond to questions about zoos and conservation.

Although Sue Goldberg's mother was afraid of cats and dogs, there were always books about animals, toy animals to play with, and small birds and tropical fish in her childhood home. Visits to the zoo and summers spent in Connecticut and New Jersey also fostered Sue's love of animals. Her other love, Yankee baseball, developed when she was a young adult. Ms. Goldberg eventually became a teacher, a career chosen when she was six, then went on to work at The International Wildlife Conservation Park at the Bronx Zoo. She soon discovered that it was pretty easy to wander just down the road to watch the Yankees. "Both of my kids pretty much grew up at the zoo. They not only spent time observing animals, they also helped me with my work there."

The book *Dear Bronx Zoo* emerged naturally from Sue's and her co-author's experiences at the park. Sue and her adult children still visit wildlife parks and attend baseball games together. Ms. Goldberg, however, makes one thing perfectly clear, "Both of my kids know enough to check the baseball or hockey schedules now before they try to call home."

Constance C. Greene

▲▼▲

Born: October 27, 1924
Address: c/o Viking Penguin
c/o Harcourt Brace

Selected Titles
1993 - Nora Maybe a Ghost Story
1993 - Odds on Oliver
1989 - Al's Blind Date
1988 - Isabelle and Little Orphan Frannie
1988 - Monday I Love You
1986 - Just Plain Al
1986 - The Love Letters of J. Timothy Owen
1984 - Isabelle Shows Her Stuff
1981 - Double-Dare O'Toole
1980 - Dotty's Suitcase
1979 - Your Old Pal, Al
1976 - Beat the Turtle Drum
1975 - I Know You, Al
1972 - Isabelle the Itch
1969 - A Girl Called Al

Comments and suggestions are welcomed by Ms. Greene.

Connie Greene grew up in a family of newspaper people, including her grandfather, her mother and father, and now her daughter. Early on, Ms. Greene had short stories printed in the *New York Daily News*, where her parents worked. Later, she became a reporter for the *Associated Press*. So, becoming a novelist was just a natural progression. Her first book for children, *A Girl Called Al*, was published in 1968. It was critically acclaimed and was named a Notable by the American Library Association.

Ms. Greene says, "The thing about writing books for children that intrigues me the most is that the children keep coming. A child who might have read one of my books when she was a child is now grown, maybe even a mother herself. I hope that this person reads my book, one she loves and remembers, to her own child, who will also remember it fondly. It is important for one's books to be remembered, for if they're remembered and read, they live."

Janet Greeson

Born: August 14, 1952
Address: 930 California
　　　　　Fayetteville, AR 72701
E-mail: jgreeson@comp.uavk.edu

Selected Titles

1998 - Name That Book! Questions and Answers
　　　　on Outstanding Children's Books, 2nd
　　　　edition
1992 - An American Army of Two
1990 - The Stingy Baker
1989 - Kenny Wild's Hair
1986 - Name That Book! Questions and Answers
　　　　on Outstanding Children's Books

Janet Greeson welcomes comments about her books.

Janet Greeson had to read 830 children's books in order to write *Name That Book!* with Karen Taha. "Fortunately," she says, "I enjoy reading children's books. There are many excellent children's books available, with depth, range, and authorship comparable to books in any other area of publishing." Janet enjoys writing humorous books that make children laugh out loud.

Still a resident of the town where she was born, she and her husband bought their house from Bill and Hillary Clinton when the President was still governor of Arkansas. In fact, the Clintons were married in the Greesons' living room!

"I have three bichons named Max, Molly, and Leo. They are more spoiled than yacht poodles," Ms. Greeson shares. "My husband and I just returned from our first scuba diving adventure in salt water. We loved it and hope to have many more."

Mary Downing Hahn

Author

Born: December 9, 1937
Address: c/o Clarion
Web Site: www.childrensbookguild.org/
hahn.html

Selected Titles

1999 - Anna All Year Round
1998 - As Ever, Gordy
1996 - Following My Own Footsteps
1996 - The Gentleman Outlaw and Me, Eli
1995 - Look for Me by Moonlight
1994 - Time for Andrew: A Ghost Story
1993 - The Wind Blows Backwards
1991 - Stepping on the Cracks
1990 - Dead Man in Indian Creek
1989 - The Doll in the Garden
1988 - Following the Mystery Man
1987 - Tallahassee Higgins
1986 - Wait Till Helen Comes: A Ghost Story
1985 - The Jellyfish Season
1983 - Daphne's Book
1979 - The Sara Summer

Mary Downing Hahn says, "I love to hear about children's lives and where they live (climate, geography, etc.)."

Formerly a children's librarian in Prince George's County, Maryland, Mary Downing Hahn now devotes her time to writing award-winning books and speaking around the country. Her critically acclaimed work includes realistic fiction, historical fiction, and contemporary fantasy. In elementary school, Mary was an avid reader and even created her own stories. But rather than write them down, she drew them because putting words on paper was boring. Things have definitely changed.

When asked how long it takes to write a book, Ms. Hahn responds, "It takes me anywhere from a couple of months to a couple of years to write a book. If I have a plot firmly in mind when I begin, the writing goes fairly quickly, but if I start with a character or a situation and only a vague idea of what's going to happen, I spend a lot of time revising and thinking things out. For instance, *Wait Till Helen Comes* practically wrote itself, but *Tallahassee Higgins* took almost two years."

Wendy Anderson Halperin

Born: April 10, 1952
Address: 76990 14th Ave.
　　　　　 South Haven, MI 49090
E-mail: whalperin@i2k.com
Web Site: www.parrett.net/halperin

Selected Titles
1998 - The Full Belly Bowl
1998 - Sophie and Rose
1998 - Once Upon a Company
1997 - A White Heron
1996 - When Chickens Grow Teeth
1995 - Homeplace
1995 - The Bedouins Gazelle (jacket)
1994 - The Ramsay Scallop (jacket)
1993 - Hunting the White Cow
1991 - The Lampfish of Twill
Series
The Cobble Street Cousins

Wendy Anderson Halperin likes to receive letters and book-related illustrations from each student in a class that has shared her books.

Wendy Anderson Halperin says, "My first drawing class was "drawing" the alphabet. Writing the letters, making perfect 'O's is difficult to do." Wendy went on to study and gain a varied background at many colleges, academies, and institutes across the country. While getting her education, she worked as an art director for various New York firms. Ms. Halperin has taught workshops for young authors and exhibited her work in art galleries in several states. Wendy's media of choice are pencil and watercolors. Her illustrations, whether in black and white or in color, are finely detailed, yet shrouded with a soft, misty palette. Wendy Anderson Halperin has mastered more than the alphabet.

Patricia Hermes

▲▼▲

Born: February 21, 1936
Address: 1414 Melville Ave.
            Fairfield, CT 06430

Selected Titles
1998 - Happy Easter
1998 - Cheat the Moon
1998 - On Winter's Wind
1996 - When Snow Lay Soft on the Mountain
1996 - Christmas Magic
1996 - My Secret Valentine
1996 - Turkey Trouble
1996 - Something Scary
1994 - My Girl 2
1993 - Someone to Count On
1992 - Take Care of My Girl
1991 - Mama, Let's Dance
1991 - My Girl
1990 - I Hate Being Gifted
1989 - Be Still My Heart
1988 - Heads, I Win
1987 - A Place for Jeremy
1987 - A Time to Listen
1986 - Kevin Corbett Eats Flies
1984 - Friends Are Like That
1983 - You Shouldn't Have to Say Good-Bye

"I love hearing from my readers about things that they care about. And I love hearing from young people who tell me how much they enjoy reading," says Patricia.

Award-winning author Patricia Hermes has spent a lot of time not only at the typewriter, but in the classroom. A Brooklyn native, Pat earned a B.A. degree in speech and English at St. John's University in New York City. Then, in the years following college and again after raising her children, she taught middle, junior, and high school. Pat continues to be involved with the educational system today, and spends much time traveling across the country speaking to students, teachers, and parents. She has also written articles for the *New York Times, Woman's Day, American Baby,* and various other publications. One interesting project of Pat's was writing the novelizations of the motion picture *My Girl* and its sequel. Now a resident of Connecticut, Ms. Hermes continues to write as the mother of five adult children—all of whom appear in one guise or another in her books.

Lee Bennett Hopkins

▲▼▲

Born: April 13, 1938
Address: c/o Harcourt Brace

Selected Titles
1998 - All God's Children: A Book of Prayers
1998 - Climb into My Lap: First Poems to Read
       Together
1997 - Song and Dance
1997 - Marvelous Math
1996 - School Supplies
1996 - Opening Days: Sports Poems
1995 - Good Rhymes, Good Times!
1995 - Been to Yesterdays: Poems of a Life
1993 - Extra Innings: Baseball Poems

Teacher Resource Books
1998 - Pass the Poetry, Please! The Third Edition
1995 - Pauses: Autobiographical Reflections of 101
       Creators of Children's Books

Mr. Hopkins enjoys all types of letters from children and adults.

Growing up in the projects of Newark, New Jersey, Lee Bennett Hopkins did not have time for books, including poetry. Survival in a rough neighborhood and supporting his family were the most important things. Ironically, Lee always knew there was only one thing he wanted in life—to be a teacher. It was in that role that Mr. Hopkins along with his students discovered the richness of children's literature. "I'd read them a poem and if they went 'ooh' when I finished, or if they told me they could feel the 'ooh' inside, I'd say, 'That's a great poem—that's poetry.' "

When Mr. Hopkins was working toward his Master's degree, the writing bug stung and he never got over it. Now an editor, novelist, freelance writer, speaker, poet, and anthologist of more than 60 poetry collections for children, Lee Bennett Hopkins maintains, "You must teach children to love books. We spend too much time teaching children to read, and not enough time teaching them to love to read."

Gloria Houston

▲▼

Born: November 24
Address: Killian 246
         Dept. of Elementary Education
         Western Carolina University
         Cullowhee, NC 28723
E-mail: ghinc@iownc.com
Web Site: http://www.ceap.edu/houston/
         gloriahouston.html

Selected Titles

1998 - Bright Freedom's Song
1997 - Littlejim's Dreams
1994 - Littlejim's Gift
1994 - Mountain Valor
1992 - But No Candy
1992 - My Great Aunt Arizona
1990 - Littlejim
1988 - The Year of the Perfect Christmas Tree
1982 - My Brother Joey Died

For my Reading Friends
With love,
Gloria Houston

    Gloria Houston likes to hear suggestions and questions about her books, her family, and writing.

    The picture books and historical novels that Gloria Houston writes spring from her experiences growing up in the Sunny Brook store in Avery County, North Carolina, and the stories told to her by the mountain people she has known over the years. Gloria's style has a rich earthy appeal with picturesque descriptive passages of woodland vistas, mountain culture, and native language. She explains, "Each person is shaped by the physical environment and the culture in which that person lives. The small details make up the richness of life. Without those details, my stories would be only slightly different from stories in any other setting." It has been a long journey from an Appalachian mountainside to the halls of learning at the University of South Florida and Western Carolina University where Dr. Houston has served as author-in-residence and assistant professor, but she has traveled that scholarly road without losing touch with her heritage. Her bestseller *The Year of the Perfect Christmas Tree* was published in Japanese and has been adapted and produced as a major motion picture.

Johanna Hurwitz

Born: October 9, 1937
Address: c/o Morrow Junior Books

Selected Titles
1998 - Faraway Summer
1997 - Ever-Clever Elisa
1996 - Even Stephen
1995 - Birthday Surprises
1993 - Leonard Bernstein: A Passion for Music
1993 - New Shoes for Silvia
1988 - Teacher's Pet
1988 - Anne Frank: Life in Hiding
1987 - Class Clown
1987 - Russell Sprouts
1985 - Adventures of Ali Baba Bernstein
1984 - The Hot & Cold Summer
1979 - Aldo Applesauce
1976 - Busybody Nora

Johanna Hurwitz enjoys letters from readers young and old.

When children ask Johanna Hurwitz how long it takes to write a book, she replies that her first published title, *Busybody Nora*, took her whole life. Soon after Johanna learned to read, she began to write as well. She copied her stories neatly, stapled the pages into little books, and had a talented classmate provide the illustrations. Ms. Hurwitz shares, "Nowadays, when people ask me when did I become a writer, I am never sure which answer to give: age eight when my friend Marilyn drew those pictures for me or age thirty-eight when my first book was published.

A lifelong resident of New York, Ms. Hurwitz took her childhood love of books and became both a librarian and an author. Much of Ms. Hurwitz's writing is geared to beginning chapter book readers. Her popularity with that age group is clearly seen by the number of child-chosen state awards she has won. She believes that every reader has a breakthrough book, a book that helps them begin to see stories like movies. Why does Johanna have such a powerful love for the world of books and storytelling? "Maybe it's fate," she says. "My parents met in a bookstore!"

Johanna Hurwitz wrote the foreword for this book.

Paul Brett Johnson

▲▼▲

Born: May 5, 1947
Address: 444 Fayette Park
　　　　　Lexington, KY 40508
E-mail: Paulbrett@aol.com

Selected Titles
1999 - The Pig Who Ran a Red Light
1999 - Old Dry Frye
1998 - A Perfect Pork Stew
1997 - Farmers' Market
1996 - Lost
1993 - The Cow Who Wouldn't Come Down
Illustrated Only:
1998 - A Traveling Cat
1997 - Too Quiet for These
　　　　Old Bones
1995 - Insects Are My Life

"I enjoy receiving letters from students, teachers and librarians who have read my books. I especially enjoy "group" letters from entire classes. I personally answer all my mail, though sometimes I'm a little slow if I'm behind on a project deadline."

Paul Brett Johnson writes:

　　Provincial America boasts many small towns with strange and amusing names. Mousie, Kentucky, my hometown, is one of them. It lies in the heart of the Appalachian mountain chain. Here, I grew up alongside coal trains, Sunday dinners-on-the-ground, and a whole lot of whittling and spitting. Long summer days were often spent with my grandfather, helping him tend to his honeybees and listening to his doubtful tales. I began to draw and paint early on. With sketchbook in hand, I spent many an afternoon sprawled on a grassy bank drawing and dreaming.

　　My interest in writing and illustrating picture books first surfaced when I was in college. Periodically during the next two decades, I found myself entertaining the thought of writing and illustrating children's stories. Occasionally I went as far as working up a manuscript and submitting it. I found the forthcoming rejection slips too discouraging and so, each time, I shelved the notion.

　　Eventually, however, the desire to make my dream a reality took over. I read every how-to article and book I could find. I wrote to publishing houses for their catalogs. I spent endless hours at the library. Then I sat down to write my first published book, *The Cow Who Wouldn't Come Down,* and I realized that it had all the elements of a good story—inventiveness, action, and believable characters—along with the tall-tale humor of a folk heritage that was my own.

　　Today when I work, I often go back to those grassy creekbanks of my youth—if not physically, then in my mind. There I draw upon a reservoir of memories, emotions, and lessons learned. In that sense, a little bit of Mousie, Kentucky, usually finds its way into each new book.

Marcia Thornton Jones

Born: July 15, 1958
Address: c/o Scholastic, Inc.
Web Site: http://www.baileykids.com

Selected Titles
1999 - Wolfmen Don't Hula
1998 - Giants Don't Use Snow Boards
1998 - Hercules Doesn't Pull Teeth
1998 - Knights Don't Teach Piano
1997 - Bogeymen Don't Play Football
1997 - Mermaids Don't Run Track
1997 - Bigfoot Doesn't Square Dance
1997 - Dragons Don't Cook Pizza
1996 - Angels Don't Know Karate
1996 - Mrs. Jeepers Is Missing Super Special
1995 - Cupids Don't Flip Hamburgers
1994 - Pirates Don't Wear Pink Sunglasses
1991 - Santa Claus Doesn't Mop Floors
1991 - Werewolves Don't Go to Summer Camp

Series
The Adventures of the Bailey School Kids
The Bailey City Monsters
Triplet Trouble

"Hearing from readers is always wonderful. I also like hearing from teachers and parents, and enjoy visiting schools and conferences to talk about writing."

The writers behind the best-selling *The Adventurers of the Bailey School Kids* series have something in common with the grown-ups who work at the Bailey School. No, Marcia Thornton Jones and Debbie Dadey are not vampires, elves, or even werewolves, but these authors were once teachers in the same elementary school in Lexington, Kentucky. Marcia was a reading teacher and Debbie was the head librarian when they decided they wanted to write for children. The two wrote every day while their students were eating lunch. But one fateful (and frustrating) day changed the direction of their stories forever. The kids were acting as if they had spring fever, so Marcia and Debbie figured they would have to sprout horns, blow smoke out of their noses, and grow ten feet tall to get the kids to pay attention! The idea made them laugh so they decided to write a story about a teacher who might be a monster. That first book, *Vampires Don't Wear Polka Dots,* grew into The Adventures of the Bailey School Kids series.

Now that Marcia and Debbie no longer live near one another, how do they continue to collaborate? "We use the hot-potato method of writing," they explain. "We start with a brief outline. Then we take turns writing chapters. We send them to each other using the fax machine and e-mail. When the other person has the story, we say it's their 'hot potato'."

M. E. Kerr

Born: May 27, 1927
Address: 12 Deep Six Dr.
                    East Hampton, NY 11937

Selected Titles
1998 - Blood on the Forehead
1996 - "Hello," I Lied
1995 - Deliver Us from Evie
1993 - Linger
1991 - Fell Down
1989 - Fell Back
1987 - Fell
1986 - Night Kites
1985 - I Stay Near You: 1 Story in 3
1984 - Him She Loves?
1983 - Me Me Me Me Me: Not a Novel
1982 - What I Really Think of You
1981 - Little Little
1978 - Gentlehands
1977 - I'll Love You When You're More Like Me
1975 - Is That You, Miss Blue?
1974 - The Son of Someone Famous
1973 - If I Love You, Am I Trapped Forever?
1972 - Dinky Hocker Shoots Smack!

M. E. Kerr enjoys letters from readers of all ages.

Concerning books she read as a young person, M. E. Kerr says, "When I think of myself and what I would have liked to have found in books those many years ago, I remember being depressed by all the neatly tied-up, happy-ending stories, the abundance of winners, the themes of winning, solving, finding—when around me it didn't seem so easy. So I write with a different feeling when I write for young adults. I guess I write for myself at that age."

M. E. Kerr is the pseudonym Marijane Meaker uses when she writes young adult novels. She uses the pen name Vin Packer with her adult mysteries and the name M. J. Meaker with her other books for adults. Ms. Kerr's first book for young adults, *Dinky Hocker Shoots Smack!*, was an immediate critical and popular success, later adapted for an ABC-TV *Afterschool Special*. Many years later, M.E. Kerr is grateful that as an inexperienced college graduate her lack of shorthand skills caused her to get the boring jobs. If she had gotten the good jobs, she would not have had all that free time to write.

Liza Ketchum

Born: June 17, 1946
Address: 7 Arthur Terrace
Watertown, MA 02172

Selected Titles
Titles under Liza Ketchum:
1997 - Blue Coyote
1997 - The Gold Rush
Titles under Liza Ketchum Murrow:
1993 - Twelve Days in August
1992 - Allergic to My Family
1991 - The Ghost of Lost Island
1990 - Dancing on the Table
1989 - Fire in the Heart
1989 - Good-bye, Sammy
1987 - West against the Wind

Liza Ketchum likes to receive brief spontaneous letters with questions or comments about her books or writing in general.

Liza Ketchum is the author of 11 books for children and young adults, including the recently published *Blue Coyote*, sequel to *Twelve Days in August*, and *The Gold Rush*, a companion to the PBS television series *The West*. She also teaches writing and speaks to students and professionals about the writing process.

Ketchum writes for all ages and in many genres. Her books include mysteries, historical fiction, non-fiction, humor, and four inter-related novels for young adults. Her novel *Orphan Journey Home* was serialized in newspapers in the fall of 1998.

"Whether I write for the curious beginning reader or the mature eighth grader," Ketchum says, "I am most interested in portraying the emotional lives of young people as honestly as I can. I strive to explore issues of importance to my readers, such as fairness, identity, self-esteem, peer pressure, friendship, and family loyalty."

Helen Ketteman

▲▼

Born: July 11, 1945
Address: 6307 Aberdeen Ave.
Dallas, TX 75230
E-mail: helenket@flash.net
Web Site: www.flash.net/~helenket

Selected Titles
2000 - Why the Armadillo Has Small Ears
2000 - Mama's Way
2000 - Shoeshine Whittaker
1998 - I Remember Papa
1998 - Heat Wave!
1997 - Bubba the Cowboy Prince
1995 - The Christmas Blizzard
1996 - Grandma's Cat
1995 - Luck With Potatoes
1994 - One Baby Boy
1993 - The Year of No More Corn
1992 - Not Yet Yvette
1992 - Aunt Hilarity's Bustle

Even though she has e-mail, Helen says, "I guess I'm old-fashioned. I like snail mail the best."

Helen Ketteman is the author of 13 picture books, which range in age appropriateness from preschool through 5th grade. Some of her picture books are tall tales and are very good for older children who may be studying these in school, or learning to write their own.

Helen grew up in Harlem, Georgia, and graduated from Georgia State University in Atlanta with a degree in English. She has taught both high school English and first grade. She teaches continuing education classes at Southern Methodist University in Dallas, Texas. She has spoken at writing conferences for adults and at Young Author Conferences, and has been a guest on television and radio talk shows.

Two of her books, *Not Yet, Yvette,* and *Grandma's Cat,* were recently published in Japanese, and *Not Yet Yvette* has been chosen to be included in Harcourt Brace's Passports Reading Program for elementary schools, as well as Macmillan/McGraw Hill's SRA elementary school reading program (in both English and Spanish).

Natalie Kinsey-Warnock

Born: November 2, 1956
Address: RD 3, Box 36A
　　　　　Barton, VT 05822

Selected Titles

1998 - In the Language of Loons
1997 - Sweet Memories Still
1997 - As Long As There Are Mountains
1994 - The Fiddler of the Northern Lights
1993 - The Bear That Heard Crying
1993 - When Spring Comes
1992 - Wilderness Cat
1991 - The Night the Bells Rang
1990 - The Wild Horses of Sweetbriar
1989 - The Canada Geese Quilt

Natalie Kinsey-Warnock

Natalie says, "I enjoy mail from anyone who has something to say about my books."

Natalie Kinsey-Warnock grew up on a dairy farm in a region known as Vermont's Northeast Kingdom in an area her Scottish ancestors settled almost 200 years ago. She graduated from Johnson State College with degrees in both art and athletic training and worked as a coach, Elderhostel director, and cross-country ski instructor before turning to writing full-time. "I have many passions," Natalie explains. "I am an athlete, naturalist, artist, and a writer."

Every morning Natalie runs five to ten miles and often sketches birds and wildflowers. Together, she and her husband, Tom, have built a timber-frame house and planted an orchard of old apple varieties.

Natalie's first children's book, *The Canada Geese Quilt*, grew out of her love and admiration for her grandmother and a special quilt the two of them made together. Presently, Ms. Kinsey-Warnock is at work on over 20 new books.

Suzy Kline

▲▼▲

Born: August 27, 1943
Address: c/o G.P. Putnam's Sons

Selected Titles
1999 - Molly Zander and the Deadly Hookshot
1998 - Song Lee and the I Hate You Notes
1998 - Horrible Harry and the Drop of Doom
1998 - Horrible Harry Moves Up to Third Grade
1997 - Horrible Harry and the Purple People
1997 - Marvin and the Mean Words
1996 - Horrible Harry and the Dungeon
1995 - Song Lee and the Leech Man
1995 - Orp and the FBI
1995 - Mary Marony and the Chocolate Surprise
1994 - Mary Marony Mummy Girl
1994 - Song Lee and the Hamster Hunt
1993 - Horrible Harry and the Christmas Surprise
1993 - Mary Marony Hides Out
1993 - Who's Orp's Girlfriend?
1993 - Song Lee in Room 2B
1992 - Herbie Jones and the Dark Attic
1992 - Horrible Harry and the Kickball Wedding
1991 - Horrible Harry's Secret
1989 - Horrible Harry and the Green Slime
1989 - Horrible Harry and the Ant Invasion
1988 - Horrible Harry in Room 2B
1987 - OOOPS!
1985 - Don't Touch!
1985 - Herbie Jones

"My first choice is a letter from a classroom and teacher (Manila envelope containing children's free letters—uncorrected and a note from the teacher about the book experience)."

Suzy Kline was born, raised, and educated in Berkeley, California. Now, she is both an author and third grade teacher in Torrington, Connecticut. She has had over 30 highly-acclaimed books for children published since 1985, but she received 127 rejection letters prior to the publication of her first. Suzy Kline writes about ordinary kids and life in the classroom.

Giles Laroche

▲▼▲

Born: July 1, 1956
Address: 41 Dearborn St.
        Salem, MA 01970

Selected Titles

1998 - Bridges Are to Cross
1993 - Ragged Shadows: Poems of Halloween Night
1992 - The Color Box
1990 - A Road Might Lead to Anywhere
1988 - General Store
1987 - Sing a Song of People

Mr. Laroche likes to receive one letter from a class with student book-related writings and illustrations, as well as questions and comments about art.

For as long as he can remember, Giles Laroche has been drawing. "My mother sketched and so did my grandmother. I remember sitting down with them and sketching old farmhouses and the White Mountains which surrounded our house. In elementary school, I enjoyed every opportunity to include drawing in my homework such as designing covers for book reports."

Years later, when Mr. Laroche enrolled at the Montserrat College of Art in Massachusetts, he studied many types of drawing and painting, then he began to experiment with collage and created a new technique he calls paper-relief. Paper-relief is a three-dimensional technique that allows the illustration to have varying levels of shadow lines. Many of Mr. Laroche's illustrations have seven or eight planes of cut-out paper sections that can be more than one and one-half inches thick. Giles especially enjoyed creating the crowds of people and buildings in the first book he illustrated, *Sing a Song of People* by Newbery Medal winner Lois Lenski.

Loreen Leedy

▲▼▲

Born: June 15, 1959
Address: c/o Holiday House
E-mail: me@loreenleedybooks.com
Web Site: www.loreenleedybooks.com

Selected Titles
1998 - Measuring Penny
1997 - Mission Addition
1996 - How Humans Make Friends
1995 - 2 x 2 = Boo! A Set of Spooky Multiplication Stories
1994 - The Edible Pyramid: Good Eating Every Day
1994 - Fraction Action
1993 - Postcards from Pluto
1992 - Blast Off to Earth
1992 - The Monster Money Book
1991 - The Great Trash Bash
1991 - Messages in the Mailbox
1991 - Waiting for Baby
1990 - The Furry News
1989 - The Potato Party
1988 - A Dragon Christmas
1988 - Pingo the Plaid Panda
1988 - The Dinosaur Princess

What book should Loreen Leedy write and illustrate next? She would love to hear your suggestions.

Like many authors and illustrators, Loreen Leedy has been reading, writing, and drawing since she can remember. "I drew and painted various animals when I was young, and I read all about them. I recall writing a school report about the spots on cheetahs, leopards, and jaguars, and how they differed. I drew pictures of the spots to illustrate the report, of course!"

For her own informational books, Leedy researches a topic she's interested in and thinks of a catchy, descriptive title. She sketches characters, writes text or dialog, then makes a dummy (a rough mock-up of the book). Once she and her editor are happy with the dummy, she draws and paints the final illustrations. Currently, she is learning to use her computer to make the art. "It's like a giant magic paintbrush!" Leedy says. She lives and works in Winter Park, Florida.

Julius Lester

▲▼▲

Born: January 27, 1939
Address: 306 Old Springfield Rd.
　　　　　Belchertown, MA 01007
E-mail: jbles@concentric.net

Selected Titles
1998 - From Slave Ship to Freedom Road
1998 - Black Cowboy, Wild Horses
1996 - Sam and the Tigers
1995 - Othello
1994 - The Man Who Knew Too Much
1994 - John Henry
1994 - The Last Tales of Uncle Remus
1993 - Long Journey Home, Stories from Black
　　　　History
1990 - Falling Pieces of the Broken Sky
1990 - How Many Spots Does a Leopard
　　　　Have? and Other Tales
1990 - The Further Tales of Uncle Remus
1988 - More Tales of Uncle Remus
1987 - The Tales of Uncle Remus
1985 - The Knee-High Man and Other Tales
1971 - Young and Black in America
1969 - Black Folktales
1969 - To Be a Slave

Julius Lester accepts brief questions and requests for advice from his readers of all ages.

Julius Lester became an avid reader to escape the realities of racism as a child growing up in the segregated South of the 1940s and 1950s. A young man in the 1960s, Mr. Lester became actively involved in the struggle for civil rights. Then, as photo head for the Student Non-Violent Coordinating Committee, he traveled to North Vietnam to document the effects of U.S. bombing missions. An interest in folk music led him later to record two albums and to perform with folksingers Pete Seeger and Judy Collins.

Having become an established writer for adults by the late 1960s, Julius branched out into children's literature with the publication of two books: *To Be a Slave,* which won Newbery Honors, and *Black Folktales.* Mr. Lester's first-hand knowledge of prejudice and discrimination have provided him an authoritative background for writing historical accounts of the black experience. Julius Lester candidly shares his thoughts on writing for young people: "Children's literature is the one place where you can tell a story. Just, straight tell a story, and have it received as narrative without any literary garbage."

Bijou Le Tord

Born: January 15, 1945
Address: P.O. Box 2226
          Sag Harbor, NY 11963
E-mail: bijoult@hamptons.com

Selected Titles
1998 - God's Little Seeds
1997 - Sing a New Song
1995 - A Blue Butterfly: A Story about Claude Monet
1994 - The River and the Rain
1993 - Elephant Moon
1992 - Peace on Earth
1991 - The Little Shepherd
1990 - The Deep Blue Sea
1988 - The Little Hills of Nazareth
1985 - Good Wood Bear
1978 - Rabbit Seeds

Bijou Le Tord enjoys all types of correspondence from her readers.

Born and raised in Saint Raphael on the French Riviera, Bijou Le Tord grew up surrounded by art and books and the people who made them their lives. Her father was a painter, her mother was his model, and their house was a gathering place for writers and artists in the community. By the time she was seven, Bijou Le Tord was already writing her own stories and illustrating them with her paintings. While growing up, her mother supplied her with many books, including French translations of American picture books. So naturally, when it came time to leave home, Le Tord opted for America.

Bijou Le Tord settled in New York City and focused her career on designing elegant floral hand-printed silks for such designers as Pauline Trigère, Oscar de la Renta, and Bill Blass. She also taught the theory and practice of color fundamentals to design students at the Fashion Institute of Technology. In 1976, she left the textile industry to devote herself full-time to her childhood love: writing and illustrating children's books. That same year she also became a United States citizen.

When writing her books, Le Tord is very attentive to detail, and says, "Research is many things in my work: it is an adventure, a tool to help me be more authentic, a way to learn, a means of collecting and seeing things. Reading is the greatest part of this adventure. Everything I read and see is carefully recorded within me. This valuable information comes back to me at the precise moment when I need it—when I create, when watercolor becomes sky, trees, a bird's feather. When words say what I want them to say, then I take from my 'collection' of thoughts, emotions, and images."

Suse MacDonald

▲▼▲

Born: March 3, 1940
Address: P.O. Box 25
           So. Londonderry, VT 05155
E-mail: suse@sover.net
Web Site: http://www.create4kids.com

Selected Titles
1999 - Elephants on Board
1997 - Peck, Slither and Slide
1995 - Nanta's Lion
1994 - Sea Shapes
1993 - Who Says a Dog Says Bow-wow
1989 - Puzzlers
1986 - Alphabatics

"I love hearing from young readers and teachers. I appreciate their questions, comments, and insights for using my books in the classroom."

I grew up in Glencoe, Illinois. and earned my Bachelor of Arts in art from the State University of Iowa. My early art career included five years of textbook illustration followed by ten years of architectural drafting and design.

In 1975, my love of illustration prompted a shift in focus and a return to art studies in Boston. I enrolled at the New England School of Art and Design, The Art Institute, and the Radcliffe Seminar Program. I found my niche in a course in writing and illustrating children's books at Radcliffe.

My first book, *Alphabatics*, was well received and won two prestigious awards: a Caldecott Honor presented by the American Library Association and The Golden Kite Award presented by the Society of Children's Book Writers. Three of my next nine books were written and illustrated in collaboration with Bill Oakes.

In addition to my writing and illustrating, I am an active participant in the Graphic Artists Guild and the Society of Children's Book Writers and Illustrators. I frequently make presentations to and conduct seminars for students and teachers.

I work in a studio called "Round the Bend" and live with my husband in Southern Vermont.

Ann M. Martin

Author

Born: August 12, 1955
Address: c/o Scholastic, Inc.

Selected Titles

1998 - P.S. Longer Letter Later (with Paula
      Danziger)
1996 - Leo the Magnificat
1993 - Eleven Kids, One Summer
1992 - Rachel Parker, Kindergarten Show-off
1991 - Eleven Kids, One Summer
1989 - Ma and Pa Dracula
1988 - Ten Kids, No Pets
1988 - Yours Turly, Shirley
1987 - Slam Book
1987 - Just a Summer Romance
1986 - With You and Without You
1986 - Missing Since Monday
1985 - Me and Katie (the Pest)
1984 - Inside Out
1984 - Stage Fright
1983 - Bummer Summer

Series

The Baby-sitters Club
Baby-sitters Little Sister
The Kids in Ms. Colman's Class
California Diaries

Ann M. Martin (signature)

Ann M. Martin appreciates all types of correspondence from her readers.

With over 150 million books in print, Ann M. Martin is the author of _The Baby-sitters Club_, the most popular middle-grade series in America. But writing hasn't always come easily for Ann; she has had to work very hard at perfecting her work. Though she enjoyed creating stories as a child, it never occurred to her that she could become a published author. After college, Ms. Martin taught elementary school for a while, then when she decided to pursue a career as a writer, she began as an editor of children's books. Due to the popularity of _The Baby-sitters Club_ and its spin-off series, Ann no longer writes all of the series books that bear her name. She does, however, work with the plotting and editing of all of them. Ann also has assistants who help her answer the thousands of letters she receives every year. Ms. Martin believes that she has a great responsibility to her readers, so she makes sure that every letter gets answered. "This makes a difference to kids," Ann says. "When I go to book signings, kids produce the letters we've sent back to them."

Marianna Mayer

Author

▲▼

Born: November 8, 1945
Address: P.O. Box 206
           Roxbury, CT 06783
E-mail: mmayer11@aol.com

Selected Titles
1999 - Iron John
1998 - Young Mary of Nazareth
1992 - My First Book of Nursery Tales: Five Favorite
        Bedtime Tales
1990 - The Little Jewel Box
1990 - The Spirit of the Blue Light
1990 - Noble-Hearted Kate
1990 - The Golden Swan
1989 - The Prince & the Princess: A Bohemian
        Fairy Tale
1989 - The Twelve Dancing Princesses
1989 - The Unicorn Alphabet
1988 - Iduna & the Magic Apples
1987 - The Black Horse
1986 - Marcel the Pastry Chef
1984 - Beauty and the Beast

Series
Brambleberrys

Marianna Mayer enjoys all types of correspondence, including book-related writings and illustrations.

Marianna Mayer has always known that she wanted to write and illustrate books. She wrote her first story when she was nine years old, then went on to major in art history in both high school and college. The study of art gave Marianna many images to incorporate into her work as she gradually moved from painting to concentrate more fully on writing. "The fact is that I feel more freedom to express myself using words as my 'paints' and plots as my 'canvasses.'"

Most of Ms. Mayer's books are her versions of classic fairy tales. She believes these stories, rooted in ancient folklore and legend, should be adapted for the enjoyment of each new generation. Marianna further explains her work by saying, "Writing is my way of sharing. Here I am off in the country, loving my solitude, needing that isolation in order to work, and at the same time I hope I'm sharing my work with people I'll never meet. But I get letters from people who have read my books. And from what they write, I know I have touched them. We have made a bond through words."

Anne Mazer

Author

Born: April 2, 1953
Address: 209 Willow Ave.
          Ithaca, NY 14850

Selected Titles

1999 - The Fixits
1998 - A Walk in My World: International Short Stories
          about Youth
1997 - Working Days: Short Stories about Teenagers
          at Work
1996 - A Sliver of Glass
1995 - Going Where I'm Coming From: Memories of
          American Youth
1994 - The Accidental Witch
1993 - America Street: A Multicultural Anthology of
          Stories
1993 - The Oxboy
1992 - Moose Street
1991 - The Salamander Room
1990 - Watch Me
1990 - The Yellow Button

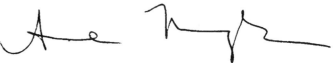

Anne enjoys mail from her readers of all ages, including children's story-related writings and illustrations.

"I was the book-loving child of book-loving parents. There were thousands of books in our house. (I counted them once, when I was ten.) No one had to encourage me to read. More often, they had to pry the book out of my hand," Anne Mazer recalls. Anne's parents, Harry and Norma Fox Mazer, became writers when she was five years old, so she grew up exposed to books from beginning to end. "I can still see the two of them in the front seat of our old blue car, discussing plot, characterization, and motivation, while we children squabbled in the back." Anne's school life was not that positive. Some teachers enforced their strict rules with blows and found it difficult to appreciate Anne's creativity. Thinking she would become an artist, Anne enrolled in art school, but after two semesters she dropped out. A period of wandering followed, including studies at the Sorbonne in Paris and work at a variety of odd jobs. Finally, at the age of 28, Anne realized that writing was what she really wanted to do. Her parents were not surprised at her decision. Knowing what she had to do, Anne got busy writing steadily and soon published her first book. Now, when she is writing late at night, Ms. Mazer wonders what kinds of stories her own children will write.

Harry Mazer

▲▼

Born: May 31, 1925
Address: 7626 Brown Gulf Rd.
Jamesville, NY 13078

Selected Titles
1998 - The Wild Kid
1997 - The Dog in the Freezer
1993 - Who Is Eddie Leonard?
1992 - Bright Days, Stupid Nights
1990 - Someone's Mother Is Missing
1989 - Heartbeat
1988 - City Light
1986 - Cave under the City
1985 - When the Phone Rang
1981 - The Island Keeper: A Tale of Courage and Survival
1981 - I Love You, Stupid!
1979 - The Last Mission
1977 - The Solid Gold Kid
1973 - Snowbound

"Me, in high school when I dreamed of writing to authors, but never did."

Harry Mazer

"Something about the letter writer's own life and thoughts are what I enjoy," Harry says.

When Harry Mazer met Norma Fox, his wife-to-be, he was 21 and she was 15. Neither knew the other wanted to write until after they were married and had children. It was not until they had been married 20 years that they each published their first books.

Harry says, "All of my books grow out of my life and my family and people I meet. But also from my dreams, imaginings, worries and broodings and things I can't get out of my head. Every book is as true as I can make it, but rarely did the things in my books happen to me. If I did all those things I'd be dead by now." Mr. Mazer also readily admits that he procrastinates when it comes to writing, that in high school he didn't think his writing was good enough, and that writing has never been easy. But, he says that writing, like playing basketball or the trumpet, takes two things: desire and then an incredible amount of practice. "Forget talent. If you practice it will show itself in time." Harry Mazer is also a vegetarian who does not drink or smoke and who avoids salt, sugar, and fatty foods.

Norma Fox Mazer

Born: May 15, 1931
Address: 7626 Brown Gulf Rd.
           Jamesville, NY 13078

Selected Titles
1997 - When She Was Good
1995 - Missing Pieces
1993 - Out of Control
1992 - E, My Name Is Emily
1991 - Three Sisters
1991 - When We First Met
1990 - Babyface
1988 - Silver
1987 - After the Rain
1984 - Supergirl, the Novel
1984 - Downtown
1982 - Summer Girls, Love Boys &
       Other Short Stories
1981 - Taking Terri Mueller
1980 - Mrs. Fish, Ape, and Me, the Dump Queen
1979 - Up in Seth's Room
1976 - Dear Bill, Remember Me? & Other Stories
1971 - I, Trissy

Norma Fox Mazer wants to hear thoughts and questions that arise from the young reader's heart.

Norma Fox Mazer grew up in Glens Falls, a small town in northern New York state. Her grandparents immigrated there over 85 years ago and established a bakery which stood in the same spot for over 50 years. "Now I live winters in New York City and the rest of the year in the country in central New York. But wherever I live, I write. There are two things in life that matter to me—my family and my writing. I write every day of the week and feel something is missing if I don't."

To date, Ms. Mazer has published twenty-three novels, three of them written with her husband Harry Mazer, one novelization of a movie, two collections of short stories, numerous other articles, and a collection of poetry which she edited. Ms. Mazer's advice to young writers is: "Start writing. Keep a notebook. Write every day. Write letters, write in a journal, I don't care what you write, just write." Concerning correspondence, Norma says, "The beauty of a letter is that it is a form for the expression of the self—real thoughts—feelings—reactions—a way to tell stories."

Norma Fox Mazer wrote the foreword "Write Me Soon" for this book.

Michael McCurdy

▲▼▲

Born: February 17, 1942
Address:66 Lake Buel Rd.
　　　　Great Barrington, MA 01230-1450
E-mail: mmccurdy@bch.net
Web Site: www.bcn.net/~mmccurdy

Selected Titles
1999 - Iron Horses
1999 - Christmas Present
1999 - Kansas Centennial Edition of the Wonderful
　　　　Wizard of Oz
1999 - Tarzan
1998 - War and the Pity of War
1998 - Johnny Tremain
1998 - The Sailor's Alphabet
1997 - The Bone Man: A Native-American Modoc Tale
1997 - Trapped by the Ice: Shackleton's Amazing
　　　　Antarctic Adventure
1996 - American Fair Tales
1996 - The Seasons Sewn: A Year in Patchwork
1996 - Passover
1996 - The Post Office
1995 - The Gettysburg Address
1995 - Singing America
1995 - Lucy's Summer

Michael McCurdy enjoys all types of correspondence from his readers, both young and old.

Michael McCurdy was born on Manhattan Island in the fair city of New York. Having grown up in New York and in Marblehead, Massachusetts, he was graduated from the School of the Museum of Fine Arts in Boston (where his roommate for a year was David McPhail, the well-known children's book illustrator) and Tufts University in Medford (B.F.A., M.F.A.). In 1996, he was awarded a traveling scholarship from the Museum School. In 1969, he used the grant to spend four months traveling in Europe and the Soviet Union. He has taught at the School of the Museum of Fine Arts, Concord Academy (Concord, MA), and at Wellesley College's Book Arts Program. He has had many exhibitions of his work and approximately 150 books contain his illustrations.

Michael McCurdy has been a wood engraver since 1962. In addition to his work as an illustrator, he has authored books. As the publisher of Penmaen Press Books, he produced significant small-press first editions by leading American and European writers and poets, including William Saroyan, Joyce Carol Oates, and Allen Ginsberg.

Michael's studio is housed in his red barn in the Berkshire Hills of western Massachusetts.

Lurlene McDaniel

Born: April 5, 1944
Address: c/o Bantam Books
c/o Pages Publishing Group
Web Site: www.eclectics.com/lurlene
mcdaniel

Selected Titles

1998 - Until Angels Close My Eyes
1998 - Starry, Starry Night
1998 - For Better, For Worse, Forever
1998 - Saving Jessica
1997 - Lifted Up by Angels
1996 - Angels Watching over Me
1996 - No Time to Cry
1995 - A Season for Goodbye
1995 - Don't Die, My Love
1995 - Now I Lay Me Down to Sleep
1994 - She Died Too Young
1994 - For All the Days of Her Life
1993 - Please Don't Die
1992 - A Time to Die
1991 - So Much to Live For
1989 - Too Young to Die
1985 - Six Months to Live

Lurlene McDaniel says, "I enjoy meeting new people, hearing from my readers, and sharing their stories."

Growing up a navy brat gave Lurlene McDaniel the opportunity to travel and live in places all over the country. Her family eventually settled in Florida where Lurlene earned a B.A. in English from the University of South Florida. Lurlene's books address life-altering events that young people face, offering both her characters and readers hope in the face of adversity. Extensive medical research is required of the author to ensure accuracy and to develop a sense of reality. Ms. McDaniel explains, "I also study the Bible to instill the human element—the values and ethics often overlooked by the coldness of technology."

The author of over 55 books, Ms. McDaniel has received many awards and nominations, and a copy of her book *Six Months to Live* has been placed in a literary time capsule at the Library of Congress to be opened in the year 2089.

Lurlene McDaniel discusses writing, publishing, and personal life when she makes school appearances, and she says, "I especially enjoy personal contact with the kids. They are dear to me and inspire my writing and story creating in every way." Many of Ms. McDaniel's books have been bought by foreign publishers, and a TV movie of *Don't Die, My Love* has been produced for NBC.

Ann McGovern

Born: May 25, 1930
Address: c/o Kirchoff / Wohlberg, Inc.
866 United Nations Plaza, Suite 525
New York, NY 10017
E-mail: amcgsch@aol.com
Web Site: www.scils.rutgers.edu/special/kay/
mcgovern.html

Selected Titles
1997 - The Lady in the Box
1995 - Questions and Answers about Sharks
1994 - If You Lived with the Sioux Indians
1994 - Silly Birthday Party Book
1993 - Drop Everything, It's DEAR Time
1993 - Playing with Penguins and
Other Adventures in Antarctica
1992 - Swimming with Sea Lions and
Other Adventures in the Galapagos Islands
1992 - If You Grew Up with Abraham Lincoln
1992 - Christopher Columbus
1987 - The Secret Soldier:
The Story of Deborah Sampson
1982 - Nicholas Bentley Stoningpot, III
1978 - Shark Lady: True Adventures of Eugenie Clark
1977 - Wanted Dead or Alive:
The Story of Harriet Tubman
1969 - If You Sailed on the Mayflower
1968 - Stone Soup

Ann wants to receive spontaneous, thoughtful letters.

"I began writing," Ann McGovern explains, "because I couldn't speak. I was a terrible stutterer when I was a child." Reading was also an escape for Ann from her sad and lonely childhood. The author of over 50 books for children, Ann McGovern writes biographies, general non-fiction, new fiction, and retellings of legends and fables. One of Ann's loves and favorite topics for writing is the ocean where she overcame her apprehension and learned to scuba dive. "I swallowed my fear and about half the ocean. I went down 80 feet on my first dive, and I thought I had died and gone to heaven. I had never felt so at home anywhere."

Though she began writing her first book when she was 21 years old, she also worked as an editor for Scholastic where she created the SeeSaw Book Club for kindergarten and first-grade children. Ann has traveled to every continent and even the North Pole researching her books. "Making a difference in children's lives is why I plan to write until I'm ninety!" Ann boldly declares.

Fredrick McKissack

Born: August 12, 1939

Author

Patricia McKissack

Born: August 9, 1944

Author

▲▼▲

Address: All-Writing Services
P.O. Box 967
Chesterfield, MO 63006-0967

Selected Titles

1998 - Let My People Go: Old Testament Stories
1997 - Messy Bessey's School Desk
1997 - Run Away Home
1997 - A Picture of Freedom (Dear America series)
1996 - Christmas in the Big House, Christmas in the
      Quarters
1995 - African-American Inventors
1994 - African-American Scientists
1994 - Black Diamond: The Story of the Negro Baseball
      Leagues
1993 - Tennessee Trailblazers
1992 - Sojourner Truth: Ain't I a Woman?
1992 - The Dark-Thirty: Southern Tales of the Supernatural
1992 - A Million Fish . . . More or Less
1992 - The World of 1492 (contributor)
1992 - Madame C. J. Walker: Self-Made Millionaire
1992 - Zora Neale Hurston: Writer and Storyteller
1991 - Louis Armstrong: Jazz Musician
1991 - Frederick Douglass: A Leader Against Slavery
1991 - Messy Bessey's Garden
1991 - The Story of Booker T. Washington
1991 - Messy Bessey
1991 - Messy Bessey's Closet
1989 - A Long Hard Journey: The Story of the Pullman Porter
1989 - Jesse Jackson: A Biography
1988 - Nettie Jo's Friends
1988 - Mirandy and Brother Wind
1986 - Flossie and the Fox
1985 - The Incas
1985 - Mary McLeod Bethune: A Great American Educator
1984 - Paul Laurence Dunbar, a Poet to Remember

"The most enjoyable letters are those that come straight from the heart with all the errors," says Patricia.

Patricia and Fredrick McKissack write nonfiction together. To make the stories interesting, they try to uncover little-known fun facts that will spark the interest of readers. Years into their adulthood and family life, the McKissacks reached a point where they felt their careers were stagnant. When Fredrick asked Patricia what she would choose if she could do anything in the world, she responded that she'd always wanted to write books for children. Together, they embarked on their new venture where they have experienced phenomenal success.

Patricia reflects on the love of story she gained as a child, "On hot summer evenings, our family would sit on the porch and listen to my grandmother tell a hair-raising ghost story, or my mother would recite Dunbar poems or Bible stories." She can still hear the voice of her grandfather beginning a yarn told in the rich, colorful dialect of the Deep South. "It was back in nineteen and twenty-seven. I disremember the exact day, but it was long 'bout July, 'cause the skeeters was bitin' whole chunks outta my arms. . . . " Patricia's love of reading and literature is also owed to the Nashville librarians who were friendly and treated her like a human being, unlike many other white people in the segregated South.

Jointly, the McKissacks have published over 80 books for children and won many prestigious awards for their work, including Newbery and Caldecott Honor Awards and the Coretta Scott King Award.

Faith McNulty

▲▼▲

Born: November 28, 1918
Address: P.O. Box 370
          Wakefield, RI 02880

Selected Titles
1994 - A Snake in the House
1992 - The Orphan
1986 - The Lady & the Spider
1986 - Peeping in the Shell: A Whooping Crane
       Is Hatched
1980 - The Elephant Who Couldn't Forget
1979 - How to Dig a Hole to the Other Side
       of the World

Hearing comments from her readers of all ages is of interest to Faith McNulty.

Faith McNulty was born in New York City and began a writing career with the *Daily News* in 1941. Thereafter, she worked as a reporter and writer for *Life, Colliers,* and *Cosmopolitan.* In 1953, Faith joined *The New Yorker* and was a staff writer until 1991, contributing fiction and a number of reporter-at-large pieces on wildlife. Her work was collected in *The Wildlife Stories of Faith McNulty* in 1980, the same year she published the adult bestseller *The Burning Bed.*

Ms. McNulty lives on a farm in Wakefield, Rhode Island.

Ben Mikaelsen

Author

Born: November 24, 1952
Address: 233 Quinn Creek Rd.
    Bozeman, MT 59715
E-mail: benmik@alpinet.net
Web Site: http://www.BenMikaelsen.com

Selected Titles
1998 - Petey
1996 - Countdown
1995 - Stranded
1993 - Sparrow Hawk Red
1991 - Rescue Josh McGuire

"Ben Mikaelsen enjoys any type of correspondence that is motivated from the heart of a reader."

Ben Mikaelsen was born in 1952 in South America. He is the winner of the International Reading Association Award and the Western Writer's Golden Spur Award. His novels have been nominated to and won many state Reader's Choice awards. His first language is Spanish. When he learned English, he had terrible problems with grammar and spelling. He thought this meant he was a bad writer. Yet, he loved to hide under the covers at night with a flashlight in his mouth, scribbling ideas on a piece of paper.

Not until college did the notion of actually being an author occur to him. An English professor called him in after class to comment on an essay he had written. He told Ben his grammar skills were those of a seventh or eighth grader. Fearfully, Ben asked if he should drop the class. "Oh, no, no, no!" the professor replied. "I just finished reading 250 essays, and only one made me laugh and cry. That was yours. You are a writer!"

Ben's novel, *Rescue Josh McGuire* is currently optioned for screen use. His articles and photographs appear in numerous magazines around the world. Most recently, he was featured on national TV with *Jack Hanna's Animal Adventures* and in *Boy's Life* magazine. Ben and his wife, Melanie, live in a log cabin near Bozeman, Montana, with a 650-pound black bear they adopted 13 years ago.

Claudia Mills

Author

Born: August 21, 1954
Address: 2575 Briarwood Dr.
 Boulder, CO 80303
E-mail: cmills@colorado.edu

Selected Titles

1998 - Standing Up to Mr. O
1998 - Gus and Grandpa at the Hospital
1998 - Gus and Grandpa Ride the Train
1997 - One Small Lost Sheep
1997 - Grandpa and the Christmas Cookies
1997 - Gus and Grandpa
1997 - Losers, Inc.
1995 - Dinah Forever
1994 - The Secret Life of Bethany Barrett
1994 - Phoebe's Parade
1993 - Dinah in Love
1992 - Dinah for President
1992 - A Visit to Amy-Claire
1991 - Hannah on Her Way

Claudia Mills enjoys correspondence of all kinds from her readers.

Claudia Mills writes:

Some writers say that they hate to write. I love to write. I write my books early in the morning, while the rest of my family is still asleep. I get up at five a.m., fix myself a mug of hot choco-late or Earl Grey tea, and then curl up on the couch with my pad and pen. I still write the first draft of every book by hand, always on a white, narrow-ruled pad, and always with a black, felt-tipped, fine-point pen. Usually I don't get much more than one page written in a day. But page by page, day by day, on the couch at dawn, I've written many books now.

I didn't always write on the couch, and I didn't always write with the same kind of pad and pen. When I was growing up in New Jersey, I wrote anywhere and everywhere—often during math class, which is why I never learned much algebra. When I finally collected all my child-hood writing from my parents' house, I had a drawer full of hundreds of poems I had written before I was sixteen. There were poems scrawled on napkins, on the backs of church bulletins, and, of course, on math tests, where the answers should have been. But I have always loved the early morning best.

When I was expecting the birth of my first child, I was stunned when the doctor told me it would be a boy: "But all my books are about girls!" "Well, now you'll have to start writing books about boys," he told me, and his prediction came true.

When I go to schools, I tell the children that they could spend the rest of their lives just writing books about the things that happened to them in fifth grade, sometimes even seventh, and, between sips of cocoa or tea, I bring that world to life again. And I love doing it.

Anne Miranda

▲▼

Born: July 6, 1954
Address: Calle Nuria 93 Apt. 2A
  28034 Mirasiérra, Madrid
  Spain
E-mail: 101606.2001@compuserve.co

Selected Titles
1999 - Monster Math
1998 - Beep, Beep
1998 - Vroom, Chugga, Vroom-Vroom
1997 - To Market, To Market
1997 - Glad Monster, Sad Monster
1996 - Pignic
1995 - The Elephant at the Waldorf
1994 - Does a Mouse Have a House?
1993 - Night Songs
1990 - Baby Sit
1988 - Baby Walk
1987 - Baby Talk
Series
I Love Math

Anne Miranda prefers to receive e-mail from her readers due to the high cost of foreign postage.

"I always wanted to be an artist," says Anne Miranda. "When I was four, my mother sat me down with a set of pastels and a glass of warm milk. She told me to dip the pastels in the warm milk so the chalk would stick to the paper and the colors would be brighter. We made beautiful vases of color flowers. It was heavenly."

When Anne was eight or nine, she saw a touring Van Gogh exhibit at the Cleveland Art Museum. "I was sure I wanted to spend my life painting. But, many things got in the way of that dream." When she was still in college, Anne began working for her mother, Mary Jane Martin, who was the managing editor of an educational publishing company. She wrote stories for a reading program and found writing to be an alternative and satisfactory way of putting images on paper. "I kept on writing and have worked on many educational programs and also on books of my own. A few years ago, I even had the thrilling opportunity to illustrate two books that I wrote."

Four years ago, Anne moved to Madrid with her family. She has taken painting lessons with a Spanish painter and has written several new books in that time. She hopes to spend the rest of her life creating images with words and with pictures, too. "Sometimes dreams do come true."

Stephen Mooser

Author

Born: July 4, 1941
Address: 1342 Wellesley #102
         Los Angeles, CA 90025
E-mail: smooser@juno.com
Web Site: www.geocities.com/Athens/
         Olympus/6124

Selected Titles
1997 - Young Maid Marian
1994 - Elvis Is Back! And He's in the Sixth Grade
1994 - The Thing Upstairs
1993 - Disaster in Room 101
1991 - Night of the Vampire Kitty
1990 - Tad & Dad
1989 - It's a Weird, Weird School
1989 - The Hitchhiking Vampire
1986 - Shadows on the Graveyard Trail
1984 - Orphan Jeb at the Massacree
1978 - The Ghost with the Halloween Hiccups
1977 - Into the Unknown: Nine Astounding Stories
Series
Treasure Hounds
The Creepy Creature Club
The All-Star Meatballs
Which Way

Stephen enjoys all types of correspondence from his readers.

Stephen Mooser, a California native, attended UCLA where he earned a B.A. degree in motion pictures and an M.A. in journalism. Prior to becoming a full-time writer, Stephen worked as a magazine reporter, documentary filmmaker, and freelance treasure hunter. He searched for pirate gold in the jungles of Panama and hunted for outlaw silver in the deserts of Utah, episodes which have surfaced in many of his books. Mr. Mooser's writing credits include co-authoring more than 250 books for reading series and authoring more than 50 fiction and nonfiction children's books.

"I don't think there is a greater, more important skill, that a child can develop than the ability to read," Stephen says. "I like writing middle-grade fiction with real life characters who encounter something a little strange, something a little off-center. If I had to describe my books I'd say I write humorous adventure stories, with the humor being nearly as important as the adventure."

Phyllis Reynolds Naylor

Author

▲▼▲

Born: January 4, 1933
Address: 9910 Holmhurst Rd.
Bethesda, MD 20817
Web Site: www.simonsays.com/alice

Selected Titles

1999 - Walker's Crossing
1999 - A Traitor Among the Boys
1999 - Alice on the Outside
1999 - The Strawberries
1998 - The Girls' Revenge
1998 - Sang Spell
1998 - The Treasure of Bessledorf Hill
1998 - Danny's Desert Rats
1998 - Achingly Alice
1997 - Saving Shiloh
1997 - I Can't Take You Anywhere
1997 - The Healing of Texas Jake
1997 - Outrageously Alice
1997 - Ducks Disappearing
1996 - Shiloh Season
1991 - Shiloh
1987 - Beetles, Lightly Toasted

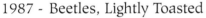

Phyllis enjoys hearing from children who are so moved by a book that they ask the librarian for an address so they can write her.

On her way to winning the 1992 Newbery Award for *Shiloh*, Phyllis Reynolds Naylor wrote over 70 books. She has been "writing" since she was in kindergarten, where she would dictate stories for her teacher to put down on paper. She was first published at the age of 16 in a church school paper and was paid a whopping $4.67.

In her books, Phyllis creates humorous, true-to-life characters who must face difficult circumstances which leave them forever changed. Phyllis elaborates, "One of the things that you learn as a writer is that everything that has happened to you, or that you have done, has happened to someone else, no matter how disgusting or humiliating or sad. And so you can draw on these things and know that you are going to touch other people."

The mother of two adult sons, Phyllis lives with her husband, Rex, in Bethesda, Maryland. She offers her view on reading material for children: "I was never a mother who told my sons that there were certain things they couldn't read. I think the only way you can differentiate between junk and good literature is to read both."

W. Nikola-Lisa

Born: June 15, 1951
Address: 4908 N. Paulina
         Chicago, IL 60640-3419
E-mail: nikolalisa@aol.com

Selected Titles
1997 - Till Year's Good End
1997 - Shake Dem Halloween Bones
1997 - America: My Land, Your Land, Our Land
1997 - Tangletalk
1996 - One Hole in the Road
1994 - No Babies Asleep
1994 - Bein' with You This Way
1993 - Storm
1991 - 1, 2, 3 Thanksgiving
1991 - Night Is Coming

W. Nikola-Lisa

"I look forward to receiving letters from students who have read and enjoyed my books. In addition, I welcome letters from teachers and their students who want to follow up on a classroom author study."

W. Nikola-Lisa has worked with children's books in some fashion most of his adult life—as an elementary school teacher, as a language arts consultant, and, most recently, as an associate professor of education at National-Louis University. About his writing Mr. Nikola-Lisa notes, "I think my strongest writing comes when I allow myself to sink down into my feelings and explore the world when I was young. There's something intensely intimate about those moments."

When Mr. Nikola-Lisa is not writing or teaching, he is out visiting schools where, drawing upon his musical, theatrical, and storytelling skills, he shares his love of books and personal writing experiences. Mr. Nikola-Lisa lives in Chicago with his family.

Joan Lowery Nixon

Author

Born: February 3, 1927
Address: 10215 Cedar Creek Dr.
          Houston, TX 77042

Selected Titles
1998 - The Haunting
1996 - Search for the Shadowman
1994 - Shadowmaker
1994 - Will You Give Me a Dream?
1994 - When I Am Eight
1993 - The Name of the Game Was Murder
1992 - Deadly Promise
1992 - The Weekend Was Murder!
1991 - High Trail to Danger
1989 - Whispers from the Dead
1987 - The Other Side of Dark
1986 - The House on Hackman's Hill
1985 - The Stalker
1985 - The Ghosts of Now
1980 - The Kidnapping of Christina Lattimore
Series
Ellis Island
The Orphan Train quartet

Joan Lowery Nixon enjoys whole class letters with a cover letter from the teacher telling how the book was used in the classroom, and with a self-addressed, stamped envelope included.

The only four-time winner of the juvenile/young adult Edgar Allan Poe Award, Joan Lowery Nixon loves writing mystery and suspense. When she was young she discovered a radio program called *I Love a Mystery* that was intriguing, suspenseful, and at times terrifying. "Maybe I'm really a detective at heart," she says, "because much later in my life, when I began to write books for young people, I discovered writing mysteries was even more fun than reading them. Before I write a word of the story I know how I'll begin it and how I'll end it, because sometimes I plot backwards from the climax of the story. . . . "

A degree in journalism from the University of Southern California and a credential in Elementary Education from California State College have provided Ms. Nixon with a varied background useful for writing effectively for her audience. The author of over 120 books for children, Joan is also a writer of American historical fiction with several series to her credit. She has even co-authored science books with her husband Hershell Nixon, a geologist.

Matt Novak

▲▼

Born: October 23, 1962
Addresses: c/o Orchard Books
             c/o HarperCollins
             c/o DK Ink

Selected Titles
1999 - The Robobots
1998 - The Pillow War
1997 - Twelve Snails to One Lizard
1996 - Newt
1995 - Gertie and Gumbo
1995 - Ghost and Pete
1994 - Mouse TV
1993 - The Last Christmas Present
1992 - Elmer Blunt's Open House

Matt Novak likes to receive a class letter along with book-related writings and illustrations from his young readers, as well as correspondence from teachers and librarians.

Matt Novak has been making up stories and pictures as long as he can remember. Matt was raised in the small town of Sheppton, Pennsylvania, and his work reflects his small town sensibilities. He put on puppet shows for his fourth grade classmates, made some animated films with his little Super-8 camera, and acted in some plays. When he grew up, he attended the School of Visual Arts in New York City and learned how much fun it was to write and illustrate books for children. Now, he writes and illustrates books he would want to buy himself. Matt's desire is "to impart my amazement of nature's beauty to children."

Mr. Novak's illustrations have appeared in The Original Art Exhibition at the Society of Illustrators Gallery in New York City as well as in many other locations in the Northeast. Matt has also worked as a puppeteer, teacher, and Disney animator. He presently lives with his wife and their two fat cats in Florida.

Barbara O'Connor

Author

▲▼

Born: November 9, 1950
Address: 27 Simmons Dr.
            Duxbury, MA 02332
E-mail: BarbOC@aol.com

Selected Titles
1997 - Beethoven in Paradise
1997 - The World at His Fingertips: A Story about
       Louis Braille
1996 - The Soldier's Voice: The Story of Ernie Pyle
1994 - Barefoot Dancer: The Story of Isadora Duncan
1993 - Mammolina: A Story about Maria Montessori

"I love hearing from people of all ages who have read my work—or who just enjoy children's books and want to communicate with a kindred spirit. I enjoy reading letters and e-mail from children, but would also enjoy hearing from teachers, librarians, or parents. I often visit schools to talk about my work."

Barbara O' Connor writes:

I believe that everyone's heart has a home. My heart's home is in the cool, shady mountains of the South known as the Smoky Mountains. As a child, I loved tap dancing and reading and writing poetry and eating moonpies and boiled peanuts. My granddaddy grew peanuts in his garden and my grandmamma always kept a big pot of them boiling on the stove. In the summer, I caught lightning bugs and put them in a jar to light up my room in the dark. (Don't worry. I always punched air holes in the lid.) It gets so hot down South that if you walk barefoot on the road, the gooey black asphalt melts and sticks to the bottom of your feet! And there's a vine that grows down there called a kudzu vine. It grows so fast in the Southern heat that it covers up signs and telephone poles and even whole barns.

When I grew up and became a writer, I sat down at my desk and poured my memories of a Southern childhood into my stories. Sometimes my characters eat boiled peanuts and have gooey, melted asphalt stuck on their feet. Maybe they see kudzu vines covering up barns. And it wouldn't be surprising if they put lightning bugs in a jar. That's what writers do. They put little pieces of themselves into their stories—and sometimes their stories take place right in their heart's home.

Katherine S. Orr

▲▼▲

Born: October 21, 1950
Address: 1511 Nuuanu Ave. PT-100
   Honolulu, HI 96817

Selected Titles

1998 - Discover Hawaii's Natural Forest
1998 - Discover Hawaii's Soaring Seabirds
1997 - Discover Hawaii's Birth-by-Fire Volcanoes
1997 - Discover Hawaii's Freshwater Wildlife
1994 - Discover Hawaii's Sandy Beaches
   and Tidepools
1994 - Discover Hawaii's Marine Mammals
1993 - Story of a Dolphin
1990 - Sea Turtles Hatching
1990 - My Grandpa and the Sea
1989 - Wondrous World of the Mangrove Swamps
1987 - The Queen Conch Book
1985 - Leroy the Lobster
1984 - Shelley
1984 - The Life Story of the Queen Conch
1983 - The Natural World of the Turks and Caicos
   Islands

"I appreciate all mail that is sincerely motivated," says Katherine S. Orr. *"I enjoy corresponding with friendly hearts and minds, both new friends and old."*

Katherine Orr has designed logos and original artwork for various organizations such as the World Wildlife Fund. Her literary career began when she was very young. "I began putting together my first simple books (about Cowboy Hank and his favorite horse) when I was about four. I drew the pictures with big balloons to enclose dialog which my mother obligingly printed in for me," Kathy recalls.

Though her interest in art and daydreaming caused her report cards to be mediocre, Katherine soon was able to buckle down and through her studies become a marine biologist. Now she incorporates her artistic talent with her knowledge of the sea to create beautiful, informative books on a wide range of subjects for her young readers.

One concern addressed in Ms. Orr's books is human care, or lack thereof, for the environment, much of which comes from lack of education. "Well-meaning people contribute to ravaging our environment and our fellow non-human inhabitants every day without the slightest awareness of it," Ms. Orr shares. "My goal as an author is to write from the heart those books that will arouse curiosity about nature, kindle a desire to learn, and be shared by children and parents alike."

Jerrie Oughton

Born: April 13, 1937
Address: c/o: Houghton Mifflin Company
E-mail: poughton@aol.com
Web Site: www.author-illustr-source.com/
 ais_6ky.htm

Selected Titles
1997 - The War in Georgia
1995 - Music from a Place Called Half Moon
1994 - The Magic Weaver of Rugs
1992 - How the Stars Fell into the Sky

Jerrie loves to hear from readers, teachers, librarians, and media specialists.

Jerrie Oughton writes:

I am from the South . . . born in Georgia, lived in Arkansas, Tennessee, and North Carolina during my growing up years. My sense of place has definitely colored my writing. As a child I went to sleep listening to conversations taking place over and around me. I believe I must have absorbed that dialogue, that slowed cadence and rhythm of the Southern way of saying things. I'm just a Georgia girl who married a Jersey boy and our five children say they never did learn how to talk right.

The day I first considered myself a writer was after I had written a piece for a magazine about my high school teacher, Mrs. Phyllis Peacock, who influenced a number of writers (Anne Tyler and Reynolds Price, to name two). I was walking down Main Street in our small town when a teacher friend stopped me on the street and told me what that article meant to her as a teacher. As she talked she began crying. Suddenly seeing that my words could move someone to tears gave me the feeling that I might be a writer, after all. I wrote for 35 years before I ever got a book published. All that rejection hurt, yes. But it also toughened me and made me just try all the harder. With each rejection I made an effort to learn where I wasn't meeting the standard.

I think of you, the reader, when I write. I picture you reading my books, taking from them what you need. Sometimes I get letters from you, the readers, telling me about yourself, about how you felt when you read my books, about how life is for you. I read those letters with care because writing, whether it be a letter or a book is an extension of oneself and needs to be held in high regard.

Barbara Park

▼▲

Born: April 27, 1947
Address: c/o Random House, Inc.

Selected Titles
1998 - PSSSST! It's Me . . . the Bogeyman
1995 - Mick Harte Was Here
1993 - Dear God, Help!!! Love, Earl
1991 - Rosie Swanson:
      Fourth Grade Geek for President
1990 - Maxie, Rosie, and Earl—Partners in Grime
1989 - My Mother Got Married
      (and other disasters)
1988 - Almost Starring Skinnybones
1987 - The Kid in the Red Jacket
1985 - Buddies
1983 - Beanpole
1982 - Skinnybones
1982 - Operation: Dump the Chump
1981 - Don't Make Me Smile
Series
Junie B. Jones

Barbara Park likes to receive one letter from a class that has shared her book.

"Hearing a boy or girl laugh out loud at something I have written is the true payoff," Barbara Park explains. "And over the years some of the letters I've received are so terrific that once in a while I reread them just to give myself a lift!"

Barbara grew up in Mt. Holly, New Jersey, and began her college career there before transferring to the University of Alabama where she earned a B.S. in education. Then, she began a life of packing and unpacking with her husband, Richard, while he fulfilled a four-year commitment with the air force. After they settled in Phoenix, Arizona, Barbara began her writing career.

Barbara hopes that through her books, children will see some of the funny sides of life and come to realize that, even though living doesn't require a sense of humor, having one sure makes it a whole lot easier to muddle through. Barbara doesn't base her characters on her sons, Steven and David; they are grown now. But she admits that, over the years, they definitely influenced her work. "Most of their help was in just keeping me in touch with the kinds of things that make kids laugh [like] underwear, spitballs and adults (of course!)."

David Patneaude

▲▽▲

Born: January 2, 1944
Address: 12606 N.E. 166th Ct.
　　　　　 Woodinville, WA 98072
E-mail: patnd@oz.net
Web Site: http://www.oz.net/~patnd

Selected Titles
1997 - The Last Man's Reward
1995 - Dark Starry Morning:
　　　　 Stories of This World and Beyond
1993 - Someone Was Watching

"Getting letters from young readers is a perfect (and perfectly enjoyable) example of serendipity: I set out to write stories and get books published, and I realized that goal, but as a result I've discovered something both unexpected and rewarding. That "something" is hearing back from kids about my books. I've received some letters that are simply gems, and those I've hidden away in a safe place to read myself again someday or share with others. I love getting thoughtful, funny letters from kids who have read one (or all) of my books."

David Patneaude writes:

Reading was one of my favorite pastimes as a young person; there weren't many things that matched the excitement of a good book. When I decided to make a serious effort at writing, I made up my mind that I wanted to reach kids' imaginations the way mine had been reached. I've spent a lot of time around kids (I was a single parent to my oldest son for a number of years), coached youth basketball, soccer and track, watched them grow from toddlers to teens to young adults, and learned a good deal about what makes them tick (while realizing that there's a lot that I'll never understand). I have learned that kids know what they like, they're honest about it, and it's not easy to fool them. Writing for them is a challenge that isn't as likely to be faced in many of the genres of adult fiction. I wanted to try to meet that challenge.

I was born in St. Paul, Minnesota, but moved to the Seattle, Washington, area with my family when I was six. Except for a tour of duty in the navy, I've done my growing up right here (at least, what I've done so far). Now, my wife, Judy, and I are watching our two youngest kids grow up.

I have a degree in communications from the University of Washington. I've also taken a number of writing courses and attended several writing workshops since getting my degree.

I enjoy running. I like the outdoors and coaching little kids, and when I want to indulge myself and sacrifice some writing time, I still love to read.

Stella Pevsner

Born: October 4
Addresses: c/o Clarion
           c/o Archway

Selected Titles

1997 - Sing for Your Father, Su Phan (with Fay Tang)
1996 - Would My Fortune Cookie Lie?
1994 - Jon, Flora, and the Odd-Eyed Cat
1993 - I'm Emma: I'm a Quint
1991 - The Night the Whole Class Slept Over
1989 - How Could You Do It, Diane?
1987 - Sister of the Quints
1985 - Me, My Goat and My Sister's Wedding
1983 - Lindsay, Lindsay, Fly Away Home
1980 - Cute Is a Four-Letter Word
1981 - I'll Always Remember You, Maybe
1978 - And You Give Me a Pain, Elaine
1977 - Keep Stompin' Til the Music Stops
1975 - A Smart Kid Like You
1973 - Call Me Heller, That's My Name
1970 - Footsteps on the Stairs
1969 - Break a Leg!

Stella Pevsner likes to hear from individuals of all ages who have read her work.

Stella Pevsner worked as a teacher and copywriter after her graduation from Illinois State. Then, following a variety of writing experiences and four children, she decided to write a book for young people. The work was so gratifying that she stayed with the genre. "People sometimes ask if I outline a book. No. What I do is think of where I want to go with the story, and the main incidents that lead to the climax. I usually have the characters pretty well established, as well."

Born and raised in Lincoln, Illinois, she is now a resident of Chicago. Along with her avid reading, Ms. Pevsner enjoys theatre, ballet, art fairs, and visiting with her children.

With respect to her goals in writing for children, Stella Pevsner explains, "But while the teacher and mother parts of me try to inject something positive into each book, my main purpose in writing is to entertain. I would like to lead at least some children into the pleasant path of reading with the hope that they will go on to other books for the rest of their lives."

Helena Clare Pittman

Born: January 26, 1945
Address: c/o Carolrhoda Books

Selected Titles
2000 - Time Off
2000 - The Snowman's Path
1998 - The Angel Tree
1998 - Uncle Phil's Diner
1998 - Sunrise
1998 - Still Life Stew
1996 - One Quiet Morning
1993 - Counting Jennie
1991 - Where Will You Swim Tonight?
1990 - A Dinosaur for Gerald
1990 - Gerald-Not-Practical
1990 - Miss Hindy's Cats
1989 - Once When I Was Scared
1988 - The Gift of the Willows
1986 - Martha and the Nightbird
1986 - A Grain of Rice

With my very warm wishes!
Helena Clare Pittman

All reader-initiated responses to her work are welcomed by Helena Clare Pittman.

"I began drawing pictures when I was a child. It was something I loved to do. Going off by myself to make a picture gave me great satisfaction and the sensation that time was stopped. It was a magical feeling, a feeling I loved," Helena Clare Pittman reflects. Helena pursued her love of art through junior high and high school where she received praise from her peers and teachers. She adds, "There seemed never to be any question about it for me: I was an artist, then and for always."

Through teaching and parenting her children, Helena discovered the wonder of storytelling and communicating with children. As a result she began putting words and pictures together. "What a discovery that was! I now had a new medium to work with. Words and pictures together equalled one powerful thing: story!"

A mother of two children, Ms. Pittman continues to create books for children from her home on Long Island.

Robert Quackenbush

▲▼▲

Born: July 23
Address: Robert Quackenbush Studios
P.O. Box 20651
New York, NY 10021-0072
E-mail: rqstudios@aol.com
Web Site: http://www.rquackenbush.com

Selected Titles
1999 - Daughter of Liberty
1998 - Two Miss Miss Mallard Mysteries:
Surfboard to Peril
Stage Door to Terror
1997 - Batbaby
1994 - James Madison & Dolly Madison and
Their Times
1993 - Henry's Important Date

"I enjoy receiving letters from children and finding out what their interests are in reading, writing, and drawing.

Robert Quackenbush has been delighting young readers with his humor for many years. In the more than 170 books he has written and illustrated, he has created such beloved characters as Henry the Duck, Miss Mallard, Detective Mole, and Sally Gopher. He is a three-time winner of the American Flag Institute Award for outstanding contributions to children's literature and winner of an Edgar Allan Poe Special Award for best juvenile mystery. In April 1998, at the United Nations headquarters, he received a Gradiva Award for *Batbaby*, voted best children's book of 1997 by the National Association for the Advancement of Psychoanalysis (NAAP). His art is in the permanent collections of the Whitney Museum and the Smithsonian Institution. His visiting author tours to schools and libraries have taken him throughout the United States and to Europe, South America, and the Middle East.

Born in California, he grew up in Arizona, and now lives in New York City in a high-rise apartment with his wife, Margery, and son, Piet (rhymes with "neat"). His ground-floor studio is just two blocks away. There he writes his books, teaches art to children, and offers summer workshops to adults. These summer workshops attract members from as far away as Japan, Brazil, and Denmark. To children and adults who strive to enter the field of children's literature he says, in the words of Winston Churchill, "Never give up! Never give up! No, never, never give up."

Berniece Rabe

Born: January 11, 1928
Address: 724 Smokerise
Denton, TX 76205

Selected Titles
1997 - Hiding Mr. McMulty
1994 - The First Christmas Candy Canes
1993 - Magic Comes in Its Time
1989 - Tall Enough to Own the World
1988 - Where's Chimpy
1988 - Rehearsal for the Big Time
1987 - A Smooth Move
1987 - Margaret's Moves
1981 - The Balancing Girl
1980 - Who's Afraid?
1978 - The Orphans
1977 - The Girl Who Had No Name
1975 - Naomi
1973 - Rass

To share a story—

Berniece Rabe

Comments and questions about her books, family, and writing are of interest to Berniece Rabe.

As the daughter of a Missouri cotton sharecropper, Berniece Rabe experienced life with all of its rough edges. She began writing poetry and reading for pleasure in elementary school. But she was forced to hide in a wardrobe during the winter and in a tree during the summer when she wanted to be able to read. Her stepmother believed that reading complicated life and once even snatched a book from Berniece's hand and threw it into the heater.

After becoming a wife and mother, Ms. Rabe was able to earn her college degree, one course at a time. Then, at her husband's urging, she took a class in creative writing. The manuscript that emerged from that class came to the attention of an agent who eventually located a publisher for Berniece's first book, *Rass*. Several other books followed and Berniece began writing books using her grandchildren as springboards for characters. Expressing one of her most passionate feelings, Berniece Rabe says, "I feel it is one of the biggest tragedies in the world that any child be denied the joy of reading. Give me a soapbox, please."

Robert Rayevsky

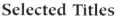

Born: November 7, 1955
Address: 1120 Swedesford Rd.
  North Wales, PA 19454
E-mail: rayevsky@earthlink.net
Web Sites: www.author-illustr-
  source.com/ais_2pa.htm
  www.altpick.com
  www.workbook.com
  www.ESGallery.com
  www.SI-LA.org

Selected Titles
1999 - Under New York
1999 - Hanukkah in Chelm
1998 - Joan of Arc
1997 - Squash It!
1996 - The Sleepy Men
1994 - Bernal and Florinda
1994 - A Word to the Wise and Other Proverbs
1993 - Angels, Angels All Around
1993 - Three Sacks of Truth: A Story from France
1993 - Birds of a Feather and Other Aesop's Fables
1991 - Androcles and the Lion and Other Aesop's Fables
1991 - The Golden Heart of Winter
1990 - The Tzar's Bird
1990 - The Talking Tree
1990 - Belling the Cat and Other Aesop's Fables
1988 - Aesop's Fables
1987 - Our King Has Horns!
1986 - Mister Cat and-a-Half

Mr. Rayevsky welcomes any mail from interested readers of all ages.

Robert Rayevsky was born in Moscow in 1955. When he was nine years old, he attended an art school for children. He holds a Bachelor of Fine Art (B.F.A.) in graphics arts from the Moscow Polygraphic Institute and a B.F.A. in illustration from Parsons School of Design. He is an award-winning illustrator of 18 children's books. His pictures hang in private collections, museums, and galleries nationwide.

Willo Davis Roberts

▲▼▲

Born: May 28, 1928
Address: 12020 W. Engebretsen Rd.
      Granite Falls, WA 98252

Selected Titles
1998 - Pawns
1998 - The Kidnappers
1997 - Secrets at Hidden Valley
1996 - Twisted Summer
1994 - The Absolutely True Story . . .
1994 - Caught!
1993 - What Are We Going to Do About David?
1992 - Jo and the Bandit
1991 - Scared Stiff
1991 - Dark Secrets
1990 - To Grandmother's House We Go
1989 - Nightmare
1989 - What Could Go Wrong?
1988 - Megan's Island
1987 - Sugar Isn't Everything
1985 - Baby Sitting is a Dangerous Job
1983 - The Pet Sitting Peril
1980 - The Girl with the Silver Eyes
1978 - The Minden Curse
1977 - Don't Hurt Laurie!
1975 - The View from the Cherry Tree

Willo Davis Roberts enjoys letters from children, teachers, and librarians who have read her books.

Willo Davis Roberts is the author of over 90 books for adults and children, 24 of them which are still in print for young people. Ms. Roberts lives with her husband David, who is also a writer and a photographer in Washington state. Together, they visit schools and speak at conferences across the country, traveling in a large motorhome. *The View from the Cherry Tree,* which was first published in 1975, was reissued in 1998 in a new hardcover edition. *Don't Hurt Laurie!,* a book on child abuse which was originally issued in 1977, is also still in print and remains very popular. Willo's books have won many state awards and she is a three-time winner of the coveted Edgar Allen Poe Award for her mysteries for young people.

Ronald Rood

▲▼▲

Born: July 7, 1920
Address: 127 Sugar Bush Hill
          Lincoln, VT 05443
E-mail: prood@together.net

Selected Titles
1996 - The New York Public Library Incredible
        Earth
1994 - Wetlands
1993 - Tide Pools
1988 - Ron Rood's Vermont
1987 - Animals Nobody Loves
1985 - The Loon in My Bathtub
1983 - How Do You Spank a Porcupine?
1965 - Bees, Bugs and Beetles
1962 - A Land Alive
1960 - The How & Why Wonder Book of Insects

Your Vermont neighbor,
Ron Rood

Ronald Rood enjoys and answers all letters from his readers.

     Ronald Rood was born in Torrington, Connecticut. As a young man, he earned a B.S. from the University of Connecticut at Storrs. Ron mined gold in Alaska until the attack on Pearl Harbor, when he joined the air force and flew P-51 Mustangs over Europe. After the war, Ron returned to Storrs for an advanced degree in zoology. He taught college biology until 1953, when a chance meeting with a Coronet editor started him writing. He has since written 30 books on natural history, several of which have been featured on national radio and television. More than 300 of his articles have appeared in publications including the *New York Times*, *Reader's Digest*, *Christian Herald*, *Vermont Life*, *National Wildlife*, and a number of other magazines. Mr. Rood's photography and lecture trips have taken him to all 50 states, Mexico, and several Canadian provinces. He and his wife, Peg, now live on an extinct farm in Lincoln, Vermont, and have four children and ten grandchildren.

Barbara Seuling

Born: July 22, 1937
Address: P.O. Box 529
  Londonderry, VT 05148

Selected Titles

1999 - Drip! Drop! How Water Gets to Your Tap
1998 - Winter Lullaby
1998 - More Wacky Laws
1997 - Wacky Laws
1995 - To Be a Writer
1994 - Bugs That Go Blam! and Other Creepy-Crawler Trivia
1993 - Too Cold to Hatch a Dinosaur and Other Freaky Facts
  about the Weather
1992 - The Last Cow on the White House Lawn and Other
  Little-Known Facts about the Presidency
1991 - How to Write a Children's Book and Get It Published
1991 - The Man in the Moon Is Upside Down in Argentina and
  Other Freaky Facts about Geography
1988 - You Can't Sneeze with Your Eyes Open and Other Freaky Facts about the Human Body
1988 - Elephants Can't Jump and Other Freaky Facts about Animals
1976 - The Teeny Tiny Woman
1975 - You Can't Eat Peanuts in Church and Other Little-Known Laws

Barbara enjoys all types of mail, with the exception of advertising and bills.

Barbara Seuling has been involved in children's books as a writer, editor, illustrator, and teacher. Ms. Seuling is a member of the board of directors of the Society of Children's Book Writers and Illustrators, and writes a column for the children's writers' magazine *Once Upon a Time*. As an editor at Dell Publishing Co., she helped create the Yearling paperback reprint line and Delacorte Press Books for Young Readers. She is especially well-known as a friend to new writers. "It is so rewarding," she says, "to see writers grow and gain confidence. I love helping them turn their talents and raw material into polished stories and books."

Barbara's ongoing series of fact books for children continues to amuse and intrigue young readers. Her picture book, *The Teeny Tiny Woman,* is considered a modern children's classic.

Janet Shaw

Born: September 30, 1937
Address: c/o Pleasant Company

Selected Titles
The Kirsten Books
1988 - Kirsten Saves the Day: A Summer Story
1988 - Changes for Kirsten: A Winter Story
1987 - Happy Birthday, Kirsten! A Springtime Story
1986 - Meet Kirsten: An American Girl
1986 - Kirsten Learns a Lesson: A School Story
1986 - Kirsten's Surprise: A Christmas Story

Janet Shaw enjoys any outpourings from eager readers.

A writer of fiction and poetry for adults, Janet Shaw's first books for children are the six Kirsten stories in *The American Girls Collection®.*

Janet's experiences as a young girl have greatly influenced many scenes that occur in her popular series. Growing up in Columbia, Missouri, she enjoyed riding horses, exploring creeks and woods, building forts and tree houses, hiding out in barns and haylofts, and acting in plays. Janet's most embarrassing moment happened once when she was writing at the blackboard in front of her fifth-grade class. She felt something fall from under her skirt down around her ankles. "My slip? My panties? I was almost afraid to look. When I did, I saw my pajama pants lying on the floor. They must have gotten caught between my dress and my slip when I was getting dressed. Everyone was laughing at me when I picked them up and ran to my locker!"

Though Janet enjoyed art immensely as a child, and even had her work displayed at the local library, she soon discovered that she was a better writer than artist. In college, some of her work began appearing in various journals and magazines.

Now Ms. Shaw enjoys being with her children and grandchildren as often as possible, and she offers this wish for the future: "I hope more than anything that they—and you—will live in a world at peace and work with others to make good lives possible for all children."

Linda Shute

▲▼▲

Born: November 3, 1941
Address: 610 Casey Key Rd.
        Nokomis, FL 34275
Web Site: www.childrensbookguild.org/
        Shute.html

Selected Titles
1995 - Rabbit Wishes
1994 - Halloween Party
1993 - How I Named the Baby
1991 - The Magic Fort
1989 - Princess Pooh
1989 - We Adopted You, Benjamin Koo
1988 - Clever Tom and the Leprechaun
1987 - A Smooth Move
1987 - Jeremy Bean's St. Patrick's Day
1986 - Momotaro, the Peach Boy
1985 - Katy's First Haircut
1984 - The Other Emily
1983 - At This Very Minute

Linda Shute

All types of correspondence are enjoyed by Linda Shute, especially letters and drawings from young readers.

Linda Shute was an only child and a latch key kid—both her parents worked—when she was growing up in Miami, Florida. At home after school, she learned to love reading, drawing, and being alone—all requirements for an illustrator's job! Linda enjoys researching the details in her pictures and the histories of the stories she retells. "I want the right flower to be blooming beside the leprechaun in *Clever Tom* and the authentic woodcutter's costume on the *ojiisan* in *Momotaro.*" Her books often include end notes with extra background. "Drawing and writing are great teachers," she says. "Each picture book I create makes me see and feel and learn new things I want to share with others." She suggests, "If you want to appreciate or understand something, draw it!"

Nowadays, Ms. Shute lives between mangrove islands and the Gulf of Mexico with her husband, mother, thin cat Lily, and fat cat Mollie.

Leslie Sills

▲▼▲

Born: January 26, 1948
Address: 38 St. Paul St.
　　　　　Brookline, MA 02146
E-mail: lesills@aol.com

Selected Titles
1993 - Visions: Stories about Women Artists
1989 - Inspirations: Stories about Women Artists

"I like to help young artists whatever their questions," Leslie says.

Leslie Sills is a visual artist deeply committed to the art education of children. "During my childhood, my creative efforts were not encouraged or supported. As a result, I never felt my art had any value, and I needed to build a foundation from which I could work. I have been able to do this as an adult and now divide my time between making sculpture, teaching, writing, and lecturing."

In 1975, Leslie founded The Children's Creative Clay Studio School in Brookline, Massachusetts. But she became concerned that the students in her coed classes knew only about famous male artists. Ms. Sills has attempted to balance the scales with the publication of her two books about women artists—*Visions* and *Inspirations*. The featured artists have not only overcome sexism, but also the obstacles of racism, illness, and poverty.

Marilyn Singer

Author

▲▼

Born: October 3, 1948
Address: 42 Berkeley Pl.
　　　　　Brooklyn, NY 11217
E-mail: WriterBabe@aol.com
Web Site: http://users.aol.com/writerbabe/
　　　　　marilyn.htm

Selected Titles
1998 - Bottoms Up!
1997 - Deal With a Ghost
1996 - All We Needed to Say
1995 - The Maiden on the Moor
1994 - Family Reunion
1994 - Sky Words
1993 - It's Hard to Read a Map
　　　　with a Beagle on Your Lap
1992 - Chester, the Out-of-Work Dog
1992 - California Demon
1991 - Nine O'Clock Lullaby
1990 - Charmed
1989 - Turtle in July
1987 - Ghost Host
1985 - A Clue in Code
1982 - Tarantulas on the Brain

"I very much enjoy receiving letters from my readers," Marilyn Singer says. *"My favorite letters are those that are spontaneously written."*

Marilyn Singer grew up in a house full of stories. Many came from the books her mother read to her, and others were told by her Rumanian grandmother, with whom Marilyn shared a room.

Although she began writing poetry at an early age, Marilyn did not consider becoming a writer until she left her job as a high school English teacher in 1974. She explains, "One day, I was sitting in the Brooklyn Botanic Garden, and I began to write stories based on talking insect characters I'd made up when I was eight. My husband liked the stories and encouraged me to continue writing. I followed his advice and soon had a story accepted by E.P. Dutton & Co."

Ms. Singer has written over 50 books in various genres since that time—realistic novels, fantasies, nonfiction, fairy tales, picture books, mysteries, and poetry.

Today, Marilyn Singer lives in Brooklyn, New York, with her husband and their pets. She enjoys dog training, reading, hiking, theatre, baseball, *Star Trek*, and most of all writing. Marilyn says, "I want to keep writing more and more books to fill other people's houses with stories just the way so many writers and storytellers have filled my house for so many wonderful years."

Roland Smith

Author

Born: November 30, 1951
Address: P.O. Box 1611
              Wilsonville, OR 97070
E-mail: roland@rolandsmith.com
Web Site: www.rolandsmith.com

Selected Titles
1998 - Sasquatch
1998 - In the Forest with the Elephants
1997 - Jaguar
1997 - Vultures
1996 - Amy's Missing
1996 - Journey of the Red Wolf
1995 - Thunder Cave
1995 - African Elephants
1994 - Cats in the Zoo
1994 - Whales, Dolphins, and Porpoises in the Zoo
1992 - Primates in the Zoo

"Roland says, "I enjoy receiving any mail from my readers, especially about their thoughts on my stories."

Roland Smith is the author of many outstanding books for children. Prior to becoming a full-time writer, Roland spent over 20 years caring for exotic animals. In his career, he has been a zoo keeper, senior zoo keeper, curator of mammals and birds, general curator, assistant zoo director, and senior research biologist. For many years, Roland was the species coordinator and studbook keeper for the red wolf, an animal that until 1987 was thought to be extinct in the world. He is a member of the US Fish & Wildlife Services' Red Wolf Recovery Team, and in his capacity as species coordinator he was instrumental in the re-introduction of the red wolf into its native range in North Carolina, South Carolina, and Mississippi. Roland is also a member of the Species Survival Commission of the International Union for the Conservation of Nature.

He has appeared on *National Geographic, Audubon, Discover the World of Science,* and *Northwest Wild.* He is the author of numerous scientific papers and he has presented many lectures for the general public, as well as for scientific organizations.

Roland photographed *Sea Otter Rescue, Journey of the Red Wolf,* and *In the Forest with Elephants.* He has been on photographic assignment for the National Geographic Society and several of his photos have appeared in *National Geographic World* and numerous other magazines and books.

Roland and his wife, Marie, live on a small farm outside Portland, Oregon.

Peter E. Spier

▲▼▲

Born: June 6, 1927
Address: 5 Wardencliff Rd. Box 566
Shoreham, NY 11786-0566

Selected Titles
1992 - Peter Spier's Circus!
1987 - We, the People: The Story of the U.S. Constitution
1986 - Dreams
1985 - The Book of Jonah
1983 - Peter Spier's Christmas
1982 - Peter Spier's Rain
1980 - People
1978 - Bored—Nothing to Do!
1977 - Noah's Ark
1975 - Tin Lizzie
1972 - Crash! Bang! Boom!
1961 - The Fox Went Out on a Chilly Night

Peter Spier enjoys all types of correspondence from his readers.

When Peter Spier's children were growing up, he would often show them a just-finished work to get their reaction. When they saw *Noah's Ark*—a Caldecott Medal winner in 1978—they remarked, "It's all right." Their comment on another book—*Oh, Were They Ever Happy!*—was even worse. "Do we have to put *our* names on the cover?" they asked. More recently, however, two young children who had just moved to the neighborhood came knocking on the artist's door. He gave them a tour of his studio, showed them what he was working on, and spent some time chatting with them. The next day, their mother called to thank Spier for his hospitality. He asked if the children enjoyed their visit and was told that her little boy had exclaimed "He was awesome" on returning home. The artist couldn't have been more delighted.

Peter is indeed "awesome" to many who know and love children's books. He has illustrated over 150 titles, written and illustrated close to 40 titles, won many awards including the Caldecott Medal, 3 Christopher Medals, an American Book Award, and the Horn Book/Boston Globe Award. But most of all, Peter loves sharing his work with others. He tirelessly tours the country attending conferences and appearing at schools, libraries, bookstores, and more.

Peter grew up in the Netherlands in the small village of Broek in Waterland—north of Amsterdam. As a child, he read a great deal, dabbled in clay and drawing, and aspired to be like his father—Jo Spier—a well-known illustrator in Holland.

Peter now makes his home on Long Island, New York, where—when he is away from the drawing table—he and his wife, Kathryn, can share their love of sailing. When asked what he feels his greatest accomplishment has been, Peter answers simply "Earning a living. I am one of the few fortunate people able to support themselves with their hobby."

Jerry Spinelli

▲▼▲

Born: February 1, 1941

Addresses:

c/o Little, Brown   c/o HarperCollins

c/o Random House   c/o Simon & Schuster

c/o Scholastic, Inc.   c/o Dell

Selected Titles

1998 - Knots in My Yo-Yo String (autobiography)

1997 - The Library Card

1997 - Wringer

1996 - Crash

1992 - The Bathwater Gang Gets Down to Business

1992 - Report to the Principal's Office

1992 - Who Ran My Underwear up the Flagpole?

1992 - Do the Funky Pickle

1991 - There's a Girl in My Hammerlock

1991 - Fourth Grade Rats

1990 - Maniac Magee

1990 - The Bathwater Gang

1988 - Dump Days

1986 - Jason and Marceline

1985 - Night of the Whale

1984 - Who Put That Hair in My Toothbrush?

1982 - Space Station Seventh Grade

"I'd rather not tell [my readers] how to respond, what to ask, what I find interesting. If I did, I doubt I would have gotten some of the incredible and hilarious letters I have. They didn't tell me how to write my books. I won't tell them how to respond," says Jerry Spinelli.

"I became a kid's writer by accident," says Jerry Spinelli. "It all started when someone swiped the leftover chicken I was saving for lunch from the fridge. I stormed to work, closed my office door, and jotted down the incident. That scene soon became the opening to *Space Station Seventh Grade*. I'd intended the book for adults, a hardback, but my publisher sent it to the kids' department." That incident turned out to be a blessing in disguise for Jerry Spinelli, the 1991 Newbery Medalist.

Jerry did not write very much when he was a boy; his main focus was sports—football, basketball, baseball, and track. Mr. Spinelli gets many of his ideas for characters from people he meets. "Once I visited a school and met an interesting girl. She carried her whole collection of books to school every day in a suitcase because her little brothers and sisters and pets used to mess up her books. She became Amanda Beale in *Maniac Magee*. I gave her my address and asked her to write to me, but she never did. So I never got to tell her that she became a character in the book that won the Newbery!"

Barbara Steiner

▲▼▲

Born: November 3, 1934
Address: 3584 Kirkwood Pl.
　　　　　Boulder, CO 80304

Selected Titles
1996 - The Coffin
1996 - Spring Break
1995 - The Mummy
1993 - Night Cries
1993 - The Phantom
1992 - Dreamstalker
1991 - Journal Keeping with Young People
1991 - Dolby and the Woof-Off
1990 - Ghost Cave
1988 - Tessa
1988 - Whale Brother
1986 - Oliver Dibbs and the Dinosaur Cause
1985 - Oliver Dibbs to the Rescue!

"I like a letter telling me which book you read and why you liked it (or didn't!)," Barbara Steiner explains. "I like you to ask questions. What do you want to know about being an author?"

Author Barbara Steiner has written over 50 books for kids in the past 25 years. Born in Dardanelle, Arkansas, she now resides in Boulder, Colorado. "In every yard where we lived I had a rope swing, and I spent many hours swingin' and dreamin'," Barbara says in her soft southern accent. "Of course, that meant I was in trouble often and my mother scolded me, as she didn't feel swinging and dreaming were a proper occupation for a young lady, and besides it didn't accomplish anything. By nine I was using those dreams to write my own poems and stories."

Early in her writing career, Ms. Steiner published books about animals. Today her titles include all types of fiction, especially mystery, suspense, and horror. Ms. Steiner's day begins around eight or nine o'clock in the morning because she tries to complete a chapter every day. "I used to write things out on paper, but now I use a computer. When I wrote by hand the manuscript had to be typed before it went to an editor. So, writing on the computer saves a step." Barbara Steiner strongly encourages children who want to be writers to start with a journal and write every day.

Anastasia Suen

Author

▲▼▲

Born: January 22, 1956
Address: 1804 Windermere Dr.
Plano, TX 75093
E-mail: forsuens@flash.net
Web Site: http://www.flash.net/~forsuens

Selected Titles
2000 - Air Show
1999 - Delivery
1998 - Window Music
1998 - Baby Born
1997 - Man on the Moon

"Send me an e-mail or a letter, so I can send YOU an e-mail or a letter!"

Anastasia Suen writes:

My mother played the radio from sunup to sundown when I was a child, and we went to the library every week. Music and words, words and music, I began writing poetry when I was eleven. The ideas for my poems and books came from my family. My father worded at Cape Canaveral in the early NASA days. *Man on the Moon* recounts the *Apollo 11* mission. My grandfather worked for the railroad. *Window Music* takes us on a train ride. I wrote *Baby Born*, a celebration of a baby's first year, using my daughter's baby calendar. The idea for *Delivery*, a book about how things get delivered, came to me on the freeway when I was driving to visit my brother. My other grandfather built the P-51 Mustang airplane. *Air Show* showcases the history of flight.

As a credentialed teacher, I have worked in the classroom with children of all ages. Now, I work behind-the-scenes to help make the books you use at school. Sometimes, I write the books that you use in the classroom. Sometimes, I select the poems that you see in your school books. I love exploring new ideas. How about you?

Jane Sutton

▲▼▲

Born: May 11, 1950
Address: 11 Mason St.
        Lexington, MA 02421

Selected Titles
1988 - Definitely Not Sexy
1984 - Not Even Mrs. Mazursky
1983 - Confessions of an Orange Octopus
1981 - Me and the Weirdos
1979 - What Should a Hippo Wear?

Jane Sutton likes to hear comments and questions from her readers of all ages.

Jane Sutton infuses a lot of humor in her writing; of course it probably comes naturally to someone who was elected class comedian. She has enjoyed writing as long as she can remember, and she feels fortunate that she had elementary school teachers who encouraged her. Jane graduated magna cum laude from Brandeis University in 1972, and three years later married Alan Ticotsky a fellow Brandeis student. She has worked as a newspaper reporter and advertising copywriter, and now teaches creative writing to special education students. "I enjoy writing for children," Ms. Sutton says. "It's satisfying to me to invent situations they can identify with and to share whatever knowledge I have gained of the world. Also, in children's works I can express a strong moral message . . . without having to couch it in cryptic language that the adult reader can feel that successful deciphering."

Jane's interests include bike riding, tennis, and talking to children about writing.

Theodore Taylor

▲▼▲

Born: June 23, 1921
Address: c/o Harcourt Brace

Selected Titles
1998 - The Flight of Jesse Leroy Brown
1996 - Rogue Wave and Other Red-Blooded Sea
     Stories
1995 - The Bomb
1994 - Sweet Friday Island
1993 - Timothy of the Cay: A Prequel-Sequel
1991 - Tuck Triumphant
1991 - The Weirdo
1992 - Maria: A Christmas Story
1989 - Monocolo
1989 - Sniper
1988 - The Hostage
1982 - *H.M.S. Hood* Versus *Bismarck:*
     The Battleship Battle
1981 - The Trouble with Tuck
1977 - A Shepherd Watches, a Shepherd Sings
1973 - The Maldonado Miracle
1971 - Air Raid—Pearl Harbor!
     The Story of December 7, 1941
1971 - The Children's War
1969 - The Cay
Series
Hatteras Banks trilogy

Ted Taylor prefers brief letters from children, teachers, librarians, or whole classes with comments or questions about specific books.

When Theodore Taylor was 13 years old, he got his first writing job reporting the week's athletics at his high school for the *Portsmouth Star.* He went on to work for NBC Radio and Paramount Pictures, serve in the U.S. Merchant Marine and Navy, and work at many other odd jobs. "Not realizing it, I was training to become a writer, a worker in words. I tell aspiring young writers to do diverse things, to go to as many places as possible, to watch and listen."

When Mr. Taylor was in Hollywood working on a motion picture, his kids were always asking questions about how stunts and scenes were filmed, so he wrote *People Who Make Movies.* "After writing the book, I received more than 3,000 letters from young readers. Writing adult books, I maybe got ten letters. I thought, maybe there was something to this." There was. Mr. Taylor's encore was *The Cay,* a bestseller, multiple award-winner, and controversial modern classic about racial prejudice. Finally, after more than 20 years and over 200,000 letters later, Theodore Taylor has published *Timothy of the Cay,* a prequel-sequel told in alternating chapters, a tribute to his most renowned work.

Valerie Tripp

Author

▲▼▲

Born: September 12, 1951
Address: c/o Pleasant Co.

Selected Titles

1998 - Happy Birthday, Josefina! A Springtime Story
1998 - Josefina Saves the Day: A Summer Story
1998 - Changes for Josefina: A Winter Story
1997 - Meet Josefina: An American Girl
1997 - Josefina Learns a Lesson: A School Story
1997 - Josefina's Surprise: A Christmas Story
1992 - Happy Birthday, Felicity! A Springtime Story
1992 - Felicity Saves the Day: A Summer Story
1992 - Changes for Felicity: A Winter Story
1991 - Meet Felicity: An American Girl
1991 - Felicity Learns a Lesson: A School Story
1991 - Felicity's Surprise: A Christmas Story
1988 - Changes for Samantha: A Winter Story
1988 - Happy Birthday, Molly! A Springtime Story
1988 - Molly Saves the Day: A Summer Story
1988 - Changes for Molly: A Winter Story

"Whenever I answer a letter from a reader, I feel as though I am completing a circle of communication started by one of my stories."

Valerie Tripp writes:

Read. That's what I tell people who ask me what they should do to become a writer. Read and let the pleasure of reading delight you. Walk right straight into the stories you read and let them work their magic on you. As you are reading, you will be learning how to write. Read everything, anything, as much as your can—just read.

My father read aloud to my sisters and my brother and me at night, before we went to sleep. He'd stretch out on the bed, and we'd surround him as he read *Charlotte's Web, Madeline, Beezus and Ramona, The Secret Garden, Cinderella,* and hundreds of other stories.

Mt. Kisco Elementary School was a wonderful old school with glass cases full of stuffed birds in the hallways and new books everywhere. The classrooms had tall windows, rows of desks, and maps and bulletin boards; they looked very much as I imagined Molly's classroom to look in *Molly Learns a Lesson.* I was lucky because in my class there were children from all over the world—Italy, Ireland, Bolivia, Greece, Finland, Latvia, and Japan. We learned words from each other's languages as Josefina and Patrick do in *Josefina Saves the Day.*

My hope for my daughter and for all of you is that you will find something you love to do. I wish a passion for you. That is, I hope you can find something—a sport, a hobby, a talent, a form of work—that you love and that gives you back the energy you put into it. That is what writing is for me.

Bill Wallace

Born: August 1, 1947
Address: R.R. 1, Box 91
           Chickasha, OK 73018

Selected Titles

1998 - Upchuck and the Rotten Willy
1998 - Upchuck and the Rotten Willy—The Great
       Escape
1997 - The Final Freedom
1997 - Aloha Summer
1995 - Watchdog and the Coyotes
1996 - Journey into Terror
1994 - True Friends
1994 - Blackwater Swamp
1993 - Never Say Quit
1992 - The Biggest Klutz in Fifth Grade
1992 - Buffalo Gal
1991 - Totally Disgusting
1990 - The Christmas Spurs
1989 - Danger in Quicksand Swamp
1989 - Snot Stew
1988 - Beauty
1987 - Red Dog
1987 - Danger on Panther Peak
1986 - Ferret in the Bedroom, Lizards in the Fridge

Bill Wallace

Bill Wallace prefers to receive letters from a whole class mailed in one envelope rather than sporadically over a period of weeks.

Bill Wallace's first year as a teacher was pretty rough until one of his students convinced him that he was supposed to read to them. He read them his childhood favorite, *Old Yeller*, and they loved it. When he had difficulty finding a follow-up book they would sit still for, he decided to write new stories for the sake of survival. Bill's students loved his stories and persuaded him to send his manuscripts to somebody to make them "real books."

Mr. Wallace continued as a classroom teacher for six years, then he became principal of the same school he attended as a boy in Chickasha, Oklahoma. After ten years of frustration and rejection, Bill's book *A Dog Called Kitty* was published. *Kitty* and many of Bill Wallace's other books have won multiple child-chosen state awards, proof that other students enjoy his books also. "Some of the most gratifying letters I receive come from teachers who tell me that my stories have helped a student with reading problems become a reader," Bill says. "I have found that reading aloud to students is one of the strongest motivational tools we have in creating a love of reading. The better job we do of teaching reading in the elementary schools, the better chance of success a student has—not only in school, but in life."

Hans Wilhelm

▲▼▲

Born: September 21, 1945
Address: P.O. Box 109
               Westport, CT 06881
E-mail: hans@hanswilhelm.com
Web Site: www.hanswilhelm.com

Selected Titles
1998 - I Lost My Tooth
1997 - Don't Cut My Hair
1996 - Royal Raven
1995 - Tyrone and the Swamp Gang
1994 - Bad, Bad Bunny Trouble
1993 - The Boy Who Wasn't There
1992 - The Bremen Town Musicians
1991 - Tyrone, the Double Dirty Rotten Cheater
1990 - A Cool Kid Like Me
1989 - More Bunny Trouble
1988 - Tyrone the Horrible
1986 - What Does God Do?
1985 - I'll Always Love You
1985 - Bunny Trouble
1983 - The Trapp Family Books
Series
"DINOFOUR" (written by Steve Metzger)

Hans Wilhelm enjoys all types of correspondence from his readers, including student book-related writings and illustrations.

When Hans Wilhelm was a boy growing up in Bremen, Germany, he spent a lot of time playing in the woods, watching animals, and creating art. "I found great comfort in drawing," Hans recalls. "It must have been my way of dealing with my fears and fantasies."

Following his studies in art and business, his work took him to South Africa, where he lived for many years. He traveled for three years around the world and lived in many countries in Asia, South Pacific, and Europe. Hans finally moved to America where he has written over 100 books which have been published in all major languages around the world. Many of his books have won awards and prizes.

Today, Hans still travels a lot and visits schools in many different countries. If you want to know more about his work and his latest books, Hans invites you to check out his web site. It's full of fun activities, contests, news on his TV shows, school visits, and lots more.

Mike Wimmer

▲▽▲

Born: March 22, 1961
Address: 3905 Nicole Cr.
Norman, OK 73072
Web Site: www.mikewimmer.com

Selected Titles
1998 - Homerun
1994 - All the Places to Love
1991 - Flight: The Journey of Charles Lindbergh
1990 - Train Song
1988 - A Taste of Blackberries
1988 - Staying Nine
1987 - Seven Silly Circles
1986 - Split Sisters

Mike Wimmer enjoys reader-initiated mail with comments and questions about himself and his work.

"I started drawing at a very early age, with people being my chief interest, whether it be cowboys and Indians, heroes from the great Bible epics, or just from my own imagination," Mike Wimmer explains. "Achieving the realism of emotion, expression, movement, and setting were and still are my preeminent goal."

Mike was born in Muskogee, Oklahoma, where his artistic development was nourished by comic books and boys' adventure stories supplied by his parents, who had no knowledge or understanding of such things. But it kept him active, out of trouble, and, above all, quiet. After his formal training at the University of Oklahoma and as an apprentice to Don Ivan Punchatz in Arlington, Texas, Mike returned to Norman, Oklahoma, so his wife and childhood sweetheart, Carmelita, could finish her studies in early childhood education. Mr. Wimmer has been working professionally since 1983 with clients that include: American Airlines, Disney, Milton Bradley, Kimberly Clark, *Reader's Digest*, and many prominent publishing houses. Mike travels for book signings and school visits, spreading his belief that, "Words are the wings of an imagination, but pictures are the final destination."

Kay Winters

▲▼▲

Born: October 5, 1936
Address: P.O. Box 339
        Richlandtown, PA 18955

Selected Titles
2002 - Abe Lincoln
2000 - Tiger Trail
1999 - Who's Haunting the Teeny Tiny Ghost?
1999 - How Will the Easter Bunny Know?
1998 - Where Are the Bears?
1997 - Wolf Watch
1997 - The Teeny Tiny Ghost
1996 - Did You See What I Saw? Poems about School

Kay Winters

"I have always loved walking down our long lane to the mailbox to see what's waiting! I love hearing from children, teachers, and librarians!"

Kay Winters writes:

I have always wanted to write children's books. In 1992, I left my job as a teacher in a public school and began writing full time. I write because I love to learn. One of the exciting fringe benefits of being a writer is being able to learn what you care about. I am interested in so many things: nature, people, history, humor, emotions. I love spending time finding out about animals, their family life, their survival skills. I enjoy thinking about how people face their fears, show their feelings, cope with the joy and pain of life. I like going backwards in time and looking at how people lived long ago, what their days were like, what were their fears, their dreams? Travel is a keen interest. My husband and I have ridden elephants in Thailand, done a walking tour in England. I have flown in a small plane over the Himalayan mountains in Nepal, and ridden a horse around the pyramids in Egypt. I have worked with children and teachers in India, Egypt, Nepal, Italy, Jordan, Israel, and Greece. But most of all, I love to read, I love to learn, I love to write!

Jane Yolen

Born: February 11, 1939
Address: P.O. Box 27
             Hatfield, MA 01038
E-mail: janeyolen@aol.com

Selected Titles
1998 - Armageddon Summer
1997 - Merlin
1994 - Sacred Places
1994 - Camelot
1994 - The Girl in the Golden Bower
1993 - Grandad Bill's Song
1993 - Here There Be Dragons
1992 - A Letter from Phoenix Farm
1992 - Letting Swift River Go
1991 - Hark! A Christmas Sampler
1988 - The Devil's Arithmetic
1987 - Owl Moon
1981 - Sleeping Ugly
1980 - Commander Toad in Space
1974 - The Girl Who Cried Flowers and Other Tales
1972 - The Girl Who Loved the Wind

Jane Yolen says, "I prefer letters generated out of real interest and admiration."

The author of over 200 books for young readers, Jane Yolen has been writing since she was in first grade where she wrote the class musical about vegetables. Jane was the lead carrot, and the finale was a great salad.

So many of Jane's books deal with the fantastic that some people may wonder if she believes in magic. "I believe that everything around us is touched by magic if we just look long enough and deep enough. I never met an angel, but I believe in the angelic experience whenever I come upon someone who is incredibly loving and good. I never met a dragon, but I have met fire-breathing humans whose words seem to poison the very air . . . We all have five senses—sight, hearing, touch, taste, smell. But storytellers and children seem to have one sense more and that is the sense of wonder."

In addition to writing in virtually every genre, Dr. Yolen's talents include editing, songwriting, storytelling, lecturing, and baking bread. Jane admits, "I read everything out loud. So I think, instead of seeing pictures, I am hearing the story as music." A multiple award-winner, Jane Yolen is the author of *Owl Moon* which won the 1988 Caldecott Medal.

Appendices

Addresses of
Major Children's Book Publishers

Albert Whitman & Co.
6340 Oakton St.
Morton Grove, IL 60053-2723

Avon Books for Young Readers
1350 Avenue of the Americas
New York, NY 10019
http://www.avonbooks.com

Imprints: Avon Camelot
              Avon Flare
              Avon Hardcover

Ballantine/DelRey/Fawcett Books
201 E. 50th St.
New York, NY 10022

Imprint: Fawcett Juniper

**Bantam Doubleday Dell Books
for Young Readers**
1540 Broadway
New York, NY 10036
http://www.bdd.com

Imprints: Bantam
              Dell/Delacorte
              Doubleday

Boyds Mills Press
815 Church St.
Honesdale, PA 18431

Candlewick Press
2067 Massachusetts Ave.
Cambridge, MA 02140

Charlesbridge

85 Main St.
Watertown, MA 02172
http://www.charlesbridge.com

Chronicle Books

85 Second St.
San Francisco, CA 94105
http://www.chronbooks.com/kids

David R. Godine, Publisher

P. O. Box 9103
Lincoln, MA 01773
http://www.godine.com/children

Disney Juvenile Publishing

500 S. Buena Vista
Burbank, CA 91521
http://www2.disney.com/disneybooks

Dorling Kindersley Publishing, Inc.

95 Madison Ave.
New York, NY 10016
http://www.dkonline.com

Imprint: DK Ink

Facts On File

11 Penn Plaza
New York, NY 10001
http://www.facts.com

Farrar, Straus & Giroux, Inc.

19 Union Square W.
New York, NY 10003

Free Spirit Publishing

400 First Ave. N., Suite 616
Minneapolis, MN 55401-1730
http://www.freespirit.com

Front Street Books for Young Readers
20 Battery Park Ave. #403
Asheville, NC 28801
http://www.frontstreetbooks.com

Golden Books
850 Third Ave.
New York, NY 10022
www.goldenbooks.com

Greene Bark Press
P. O. Box 1108
Bridgeport, CT 06601-1108
http://www.bookworld.com/greenebark

Grolier Children's Publishing
Sherman Turnpike
Danbury, CT 06816
http://clubhouse.grolier.com

Imprints: Orchard Books
             Franklin Watts, Inc.
             Children's Press
             95 Madison Ave.
             New York, NY 10016

Harcourt Brace and Co. Children's Book Division
http://www.harcourtbooks.com/childrens

Imprints: Gulliver Books
             Harcourt Brace Children's Books
             Voyager Paperbacks
             Odyssey Paperbacks
             Silver Whistle Books
             Red Wagon Books
             1250 Sixth Ave.
             San Diego, CA 92101

             Browndeer Press
             9 Monroe Pkwy., Suite 240
             Lake Oswego, OR 97035-1487

HarperCollins Children's Books
10 E. 53rd St.
New York, NY 10022
http://www.harperchildrens.com

Imprints: Laura Geringer Books
               HarperActive
               Michael DiCapua Books
               Joanna Cotler Books
               Harper Festival
               Trophy Books

Holiday House
425 Madison Ave.
New York, NY 10017

Henry Holt and Co.
115 W. 18th St.
New York, NY 10011
http://www.henryholt.com/byr

Imprints: Edge Books
               Redfeather Books
               Owlet Paperbacks

Houghton Mifflin Co.
http://www.hmco.com/trade/childrens

Imprints: Houghton Mifflin
               Walter Lorraine Books
               Sandpiper Paperbooks
               222 Berkeley St.
               Boston, MA 02116

               Clarion Books
               215 Park Ave. S.
               New York, NY 10003

Hyperion Books for Children
114 Fifth Ave.
New York, NY 10011

Ideals Children's Books
1501 County Hospital Rd.
Nashville, TN 37218-2501

Kingfisher Books
95 Madison Ave.
New York, NY 10022

Lee & Low Books, Inc.
95 Madison Ave.
New York, NY 10016-7801
http://www.leeandlow.com

Lerner Publications Co.
241 First Ave. N.
Minneapolis, MN 55401
http://www.lernerbooks.com

Imprints: Carolrhoda Books
                    Lerner Books

Little Brown & Co.
3 Center Plaza
Boston, MA 02108

The Millbrook Press
2 Old New Milford Rd.
Brookfield, CT 06804
http://www.neca.com/mall/millbrook

Imprint: Copper Beech

Mondo Publishing
One Plaza Rd.
Greenvale, NY 11548
http://www.mondopub.com

North-South Books
1123 Broadway, Suite 800
New York, NY 10010
http://www.northsouth.com

Richard C. Owen Publishers, Inc.

P. O. Box 585
Katonah, NY 10536
http://www.rcowen.com

Pages Publishing Group

801 94th Ave. N.
St. Petersburg, FL 33702

Imprints: Willowisp Press
              Worthington Press
              Riverbank Press
              Hamburger Press

Peachtree Publishers, Ltd.

494 Armour Circle NE
Atlanta, GA 30324
http://www.peachtree-online.com/kids

Pelican Publishing Co., Inc.

P. O. Box 3110
Gretna, LA 70054-3110
http://www.pelicanpub.com

Penguin Putnam, Inc.

345 Hudson St.
New York, NY 10014
http://www.penguinputnam.com/yreaders

Imprints: Dial Books for Young Readers
              Dutton Children's Books
              G. P. Putnam's Sons
              Grosset & Dunlap
              Paperstar Books
              Philomel Books
              Planet Dexter
              Playskool Books
              Price Stern Sloan
              Puffin Books
              Viking Children's Books

Pleasant Company
8400 Fairway Pl.
P.O. Box 998
Middleton, WI 53562-0998
http://www.americangirls.com

Random House, Inc.
201 E. 50th St.
New York, NY 10022
http://www.randomhouse.com/kids

Imprints: Apple Soup Books
              Crown Publishers
              Alfred A. Knopf
              Random House Books for Young Readers
              Ballantine
              Del Rey
              Fawcett
              Ivy

Scholastic, Inc.
555 Broadway
New York, NY 10012-3999
http://www.scholastic.com

Imprints: Blue Sky Press
              Apple Books
              Point Paperbacks
              Cartwheel Books
              Scholastic Press
              Sunfire
              Mariposa
              Arthur Levine Books

Scholastic Canada, Ltd.
123 Newkirk Rd.
Richmond Hill, ON L4C 3G5
Canada

Silver Burdett Press
299 Jefferson Rd.
Parsippany, NJ 07054-0480

Silver Burdett Press (Continued)

Imprints: Crestwood House
Dillon Press
Julian Messner
New Discovery Books
Silver Press

Simon & Schuster Books for Young Readers

1230 Avenue of the Americas
New York, NY 10020
http://www.simonsayskids.com

Imprints: Alladin Paperbacks
Archway Paperbacks
Atheneum Books for Young Readers
Margaret K. McElderry Books
Minstrel Books
Pocket Books
Julian Messner
Simon & Schuster Books for Young Readers

Troll Communications

100 Corporate Dr.
Mahwah, NJ 07430
http://www.troll.com

Imprints: Bridgewater Books

Turtle Books

866 United Nations Plaza
New York, NY 10017
http://www.turtlebooks.com

Walker and Co.

435 Hudson St.
New York, NY 10014

Wm. B. Eerdmans Publishing Co.

255 Jefferson Ave. SE
Grand Rapids, MI 49503

William Morrow & Co., Inc.
1350 Avenue of the Americas
New York, NY 10019
http://www.williammorrow.com/wm/children.html

Imprints: Beech Tree Books
              Greenwillow Books
              Lothrop, Lee & Shepard Books
              Morrow Junior Books

Addresses of Children's Literature Organizations

American Library Association (ALA)
Association for Library Service to Children (ALSC)
50 E. Huron St.
Chicago, IL 60611
http://www.ala.org/alsc/

Canadian Society of Children's Authors,
Illustrators, and Performers
35 Spadina Rd.
Toronto, ON M5R 2S9
Canada
http://www.interlog.com/~canscaip

The Children's Book Council, Inc.
568 Broadway
New York, NY 10012
http://www.cbcbooks.org

The Children's Book Guild
http://www.childrensbookguild.org/

Society of Children's Book Writers and Illustrators
345 N. Maple Dr., Suite 296
Beverly Hills, CA 90210
http://www.scbwi.org

Listed Authors and Illustrators
Whose Books Have Won
Newberys, Caldecotts, and Honors

Marion Dane Bauer
On My Honor - Newbery Honor, 1987

Joan Blos
A Gathering of Days: A New England Girl's Journal, 1830-1832 - Newbery Medal, 1980

Betsy Byars
Summer of the Swans - Newbery Medal, 1971

Christopher Collier
My Brother Sam Is Dead - Newbery Honor, 1975

Jean Fritz
Homesick: My Own Story - Newbery Honor, 1983

Leonard Everett Fisher
America Is Born: A History for Peter - Newbery Honor, 1960
America Moves Forward: A History for Peter - Newbery Honor, 1961

Tom Feelings
To Be a Slave - Newbery Honor, 1969
Moja Means One: Swahili Counting Book - Caldecott Honor, 1972
Jambo Means Hello - Caldecott Honor, 1975

Ed Emberley
One Wide River to Cross - Caldecott Honor, 1967
Drummer Hoff - Caldecott Medal, 1968

Julius Lester
To Be a Slave - Newbery Honor, 1969
John Henry - Caldecott Honor, 1995

Patricia C. McKissack
Mirandy and Brother Wind - Caldecott Honor, 1989
The Dark-Thirty: Southern Tales of the Supernatural - Newbery Honor, 1993

Norma Fox Mazer
After the Rain - Newbery Honor, 1988

▲▼▲

Phyllis Reynolds Naylor
Shiloh - Newbery Medal, 1992

Peter Spier
Noah's Ark - Caldecott Medal, 1997

Jerry Spinelli
Maniac Magee - Newbery Medal, 1991
Wringer - Newbery Honor, 1998

Suzanne Fisher Staples
Shabanu, Daughter of the Wind - Newbery Honor, 1990

Jane Yolen
Owl Moon - Caldecott Medal, 1988
The Emperor and the Kite - Caldecott Honor, 1968

▲▼▲

Birthdays of Authors and Illustrators

January
1 Sue Goldberg
2 David Patneaude
4 Phyllis Reynolds Naylor
6 Ina R. Friedman
11 Berniece Rabe
15 Bijou Le Tord
23 Thomas B. Allen
26 Helena Clare Pittman
26 Leslie Sills
27 Julius Lester
29 Christoper Collier

February
1 Jerry Spinelli
3 Joan Lowery Nixon
11 Jane Yolen
17 Michael McCurdy
21 Jim Aylesworth
21 Patricia Hermes

March
3 Suse MacDonald
17 Keith Baker
21 Peter Catalanotto
22 Mike Wimmer
28 Angelica Shirley Carpenter

April
2 Anne Mazer
5 Lurlene McDaniel
10 Wendy Anderson Halperin
13 Lee Bennett Hopkins
13 Jerrie Oughton
27 Barbara Park

May
9 Claudine G. Wirths
10 Caroline B. Cooney
11 Jane Sutton
12 Jennifer Armstrong
15 Norma Fox Mazer
18 Debbie Dadey
19 Tom Feelings
19 Paul Brett Johnson
25 Ann McGovern
27 M.E. Kerr
28 Willo Davis Roberts
31 Harry Mazer

June
6 Peter Spier
13 David Budbill
15 Loreen Leedy
15 W. Nikola-lisa
17 Liza Ketchum
23 Theodore Taylor
24 Leonard Everett Fisher

July
1 Giles Laroche
2 Jack Gantos
4 Stephen Mooser
6 Anne Miranda
7 Ronald Rood
8 James Cross Giblin
11 Barbara Casey
11 Lynn Cullen
11 Helen Ketteman
13 Tom Birdseye
15 Marcia Thornton Jones
22 Barbara Seuling
23 Robert Quackenbush
24 Sherry Garland
29 Mary Bowman-Kruhm

August
1 Gail Gibbons
1 Bill Wallace
7 Betsy Byars
8 Frederick Drimmer
9 Patricia McKissack
12 Ann M. Martin
12 Fredrick McKissack
14 Janet Greeson
17 Carol Adorjan
21 Claudia Mills
27 Suzy Kline

September
9 Valerie Tripp
21 Hans Wilhelm
30 Janet Shaw

October
3 R. Howard Blount, Jr.
3 Marilyn Singer
4 Stella Pevsner
5 Kay Winters
9 Johanna Hurwitz
16 Sandy Asher
19 Ed Emberley
21 Ann Cameron
21 Katherine S. Orr
23 Matt Novak
27 Constance C. Greene

November
2 Natalie Kinsey-Warnock
3 Linda Shute
3 Barbara Steiner
5 Larry Dane Brimmer
7 Sneed B. Collard III
7 Robert Rayevsky
8 Marianna Mayer
9 Barbara O'Connor
16 Jean Fritz
20 Marion Dane Bauer
24 Gloria Houston
24 Ben Mikaelsen
28 Faith McNulty
30 Roland Smith

December
1 Jan Brett
6 Arlene Dubanevich
9 Joan Blos
9 Mary Downing Hahn
25 Eth Clifford

Valid Reasons to Write an Author or Illustrator

✦ You are fascinated with the author's work.

✦ There was something in the book you didn't understand.

✦ You didn't like the ending.

✦ You have read several of his/her books and can't wait for the next one.

✦ The book moved you to laughter or tears or provoked passionate emotions (e.g., love, happiness, rage, sadness, fear, confusion).

✦ You admire the author's style.

✦ You need advice about writing or illustrating and you respect this person's work.

✦ You think you found an error in the book.

✦ You've researched the author and still have questions.

✦ You're interested in the subject matter of a book and want to know more.

✦ You couldn't put the book down.

✦ You want to be heard because you have something valuable to say that will make a difference.

✦ You have an idea to share that you think would make a great story.

✦ You would like to share something interesting, humorous, or typical that has happened to you or your friends.

Poor Reasons
To Write an Author or Illustrator

➤ You want a pen pal.

➤ It's a class assignment.

➤ You want to get free stuff.

➤ You collect autographs.

➤ You want to get to know the author.

➤ You want the author to proofread your manuscript.

➤ You share the same birthday.

➤ You're nosy.

▲▼

Friendly Letter Format

(Heading)

Street Address, PO Box, or RR ____

City, ST ZIP Code® ____

Month Day, Year ____

Dear Mr./Ms. Author, ____   **(Salutation)**

_____

_____

_____

_____

(Body)

_____

_____

_____

_____

(Closing)   Yours truly, ____

(Signature)   Your Name ____

Friendly Letter Guide

_____

_____

_____

_____

_____

_____

_____

_____

_____

_____

_____

_____

_____

_____

Examples of Valid Questions

♦ What caused you to write this story? Was it a personal experience?

♦ Why did you say that Megan's father was "touched?"

♦ Why didn't Jonathan's parents get back together at the end of the book? I thought stories were supposed to have happy endings.

♦ I've been waiting a year for your next book. When is it coming out?

♦ Why do all of your books deal with death?

♦ How can you get away with one word sentences and paragraphs? I thought you had to write in complete sentences.

♦ Do you use watercolors for your paintings or do you use colored pencils and a wet brush?

♦ Why does the back cover say that Donnie's last name is Fields when in the book his last name is Fielding?

♦ I've researched in several places, but I still have a question. Did <u>Winds of Forever</u> win any awards?

♦ I really am interested in how to make the toys the pioneer children played with in <u>Prairie Days</u>. Can you tell me how to get more information?

♦ Do patients with cystic fibrosis always die at an early age, or do some live with the disease until they are old?

♦ <u>Swordsman</u> was so exciting! I hope you are writing a sequel. Are you?

♦ My cousin was ten years old before his parents told him that he was adopted. I don't think that was fair, but he acts like he's okay. Would his story make a good book?

Examples of Poor Questions

(and other inconsiderate phrases)

➤ How much money do you make?

➤ Are you rich?

➤ Will you send me a free book?

➤ Are you married?

➤ Do you have sisters or brothers?

➤ How old are you?

➤ When is your birthday?

➤ Did you like the fruitcake I sent you?

➤ Will you read my manuscript and tell me if you like it?

➤ Will you ask your editor to read my manuscript?

➤ My teacher made me write this letter.

➤ Please send me all the free information you can by Friday.

➤ If you write back I will get a better grade.

➤ My teacher wants to know if you will send her your autograph.

Clichéd Questions

➤ Where do you get your ideas?

➤ How many books have you written?

➤ Did you write when you were a child?

➤ What was your favorite book when you were a child?

➤ What is your favorite book that you wrote?

➤ What is your favorite book by another author?

➤ Who is your favorite character in your stories?

➤ Who do you admire?

➤ Do you base your books on personal experience?

➤ What other jobs have you had?

➤ Who are other authors you have met?

➤ What advice do you have for children?

➤ How do I become an author?

Poorly-Written Letter

Davy Adams 416 North
Mane St. Tampa
Fla.33555

Deer Tom:

I din't won't to right this letter but we got to, its a shcool assinment Do you got sisters or bruthers? I got three. Are you merried? Oh yeah, Hi. My name is Davy. Are teacher told us we got to right one arthur. I picked you cause you right short books. With lots of pichers. How old are you? Plez right back and send me all the free stuff and junk you got about you and plez hurry. I red all yore books My report is do on Friday. My techer sed if you right back I will git a better grade. I wont the best grade in the hole forth grade You are my favrit arthur im sorry this is so sloppy but I dint feel like righting it agin cause my hand tried. By

P.S. Are you rich?

Well-Written Letter

986 E. Bay Blvd.
Tampa, FL 33555
February 17, 1995

Dear Ms. Dalton,

I just finished <u>A Distant Time</u>, and I'm so full of mixed feelings that if I don't tell you, I think I will burst!

Obviously, I loved the book because I couldn't put it down, but I hated the way Daniel was treated by his family. First, he was abandoned and left with only a rickety roof over his head. Then he had to scavenge for food in the rubbish piles of the market, believing that he was alone in the world. I don't think I could make it if my family deserted me that way.

The scene where Daniel thought he saw his mother's face in the crowd, and he chased her, only to be grabbed by a merchant who thought he was a thief, made my heart pound almost out of my chest. The last chapter was the best, though. I thought his family was gone forever.

But there was one part I couldn't figure out. Who was the stranger who left secret messages on scraps of paper?

I can't wait to tell my class about this book. I know several of my friends will love this book as much as I do. I think it should have won the Newbery Medal. I'm going to read your book, <u>Hidden Rooms</u>, next.

I have enclosed a SASE and my school picture from last year. I think it's ugly, but at least you'll know what I used to look like. Maybe my sixth grade picture will be better.

Thanks for listening to me, and thank you for your books. I know you're a busy lady, but I would love to hear from you when you get a chance.

Your reader,
Lisa Martin

Envelope Format

```
┌─────────────────────────────────────────────────────────────┐
│  YOUR NAME                                          ┌───────┐ │
│  _____                                   │       │ │
│  STREET ADDRESS or PO BOX    (Return Address)       │ Stamp │ │
│  _____                                   │       │ │
│  CITY  ST  ZIP Code®                                └───────┘ │
│  _____                                            │
│                                                              │
│                             AUTHOR'S NAME                    │
│                             _____                 │
│        (Mailing Address)    AUTHOR'S ADDRESS                │
│                             _____                 │
│                             CITY ST ZIP Code®              │
│                             _____                 │
│                                                              │
└─────────────────────────────────────────────────────────────┘
```

Note: Do not confuse the state abbreviation shown as ST with the abbreviation for street. It is written this way just as a reminder to use the USPS standard abbreviations for states.

Envelope Guide

```
┌─────────────────────────────────────────────────────────────┐
│  _____                                  ┌───────┐ │
│  _____                                  │       │ │
│  _____                                  │ Stamp │ │
│                                                    │       │ │
│                                                    └───────┘ │
│                                                              │
│                             _____                 │
│                             _____                 │
│                             _____                 │
│                                                              │
└─────────────────────────────────────────────────────────────┘
```

▲▼

Poorly Addressed Envelope

Davy

Tom Meadows Rt.

1 box 37 Adamsville

Calif.

98765

Accurately Addressed Envelope

LISA MARTIN

986 E BAY BLVD

TAMPA FL 33555

Stamp

MS RACHEL DALTON

PO BOX 1234

BROUGHTON CT 12345

▲▼▲

State Abbreviations

Alabama	**AL**	Montana	**MT**
Alaska	**AK**	Nebraska	**NE**
Arizona	**AZ**	Nevada	**NV**
Arkansas	**AR**	New Hampshire	**NH**
California	**CA**	New Jersey	**NJ**
Colorado	**CO**	New Mexico	**NM**
Connecticut	**CT**	New York	**NY**
Delaware	**DE**	North Carolina	**NC**
District of Columbia	**DC**	North Dakota	**ND**
Florida	**FL**	Ohio	**OH**
Georgia	**GA**	Oklahoma	**OK**
Hawaii	**HI**	Oregon	**OR**
Idaho	**ID**	Pennsylvania	**PA**
Illinois	**IL**	Puerto Rico	**PR**
Indiana	**IN**	Rhode Island	**RI**
Iowa	**IA**	South Carolina	**SC**
Kansas	**KS**	South Dakota	**SD**
Kentucky	**KY**	Tennessee	**TN**
Louisiana	**LA**	Texas	**TX**
Maine	**ME**	Utah	**UT**
Maryland	**MD**	Vermont	**VT**
Massachusetts	**MA**	Virginia	**VA**
Michigan	**MI**	Washington	**WA**
Minnesota	**MN**	West Virginia	**WV**
Mississippi	**MS**	Wisconsin	**WI**
Missouri	**MO**	Wyoming	**WY**

Canadian Province Abbreviations

Alberta	**AB**	Northwest Territory	**NT**
British Columbia	**BC**	Ontario	**ON**
Manitoba	**MB**	Prince Edward Island	**PE**
New Brunswick	**NB**	Province of Quebec	**PQ**
Newfoundland	**NF**	Saskatchewan	**SK**
Nova Scotia	**NS**	Yukon	**YT**

Note: Use all capital letters and no periods with all envelope abbreviations.

Envelope Abbreviations

Roadways

Avenue	**AVE**	Lane	**LN**	Station	**STA**
Boulevard	**BLVD**	Meadows	**MDWS**	Terrace	**TER**
Circle	**CIR**	Parkway	**PKWY**	Trail	**TRL**
Court	**CT**	Place	**PL**	Turnpike	**TPKE**
Drive	**DR**	Plaza	**PLZ**	Walk	**WALK**
Gardens	**GDNS**	Road	**RD**	Way	**WAY**
Highway	**HWY**	Square	**SQ**		
Island	**IS**	Street	**ST**		

Buildings

Apartment	**APT**	Room	**RM**	Suite	**STE**

Directions

North	**N**	Northeast	**NE**
South	**S**	Northwest	**NW**
East	**E**	Southeast	**SE**
West	**W**	Southwest	**SW**

Mailboxes

(examples)

PO BOX 321

RR 1 BOX 5

Note: Use all capital letters and no periods with all envelope abbreviations.

Write-the-Author Project Checklist

- ☐ Integrate authors into classroom design and conduct author studies.
- ☐ Remember national book weeks are busy times for many authors.
- ☐ Teach a friendly letter writing unit.
- ☐ Write one letter from the whole class if possible.
- ☐ Batch if single letters are mailed, and expect one response to the class.
- ☐ Enclose a personal note with class letters.
- ☐ Allow each student to write the author of his/her choice.
- ☐ Limit the number of letters mailed to individual authors.
- ☐ Verify that each child has read a book by the chosen author.
- ☐ Ask students to research their authors prior to letter writing.
- ☐ Discuss appropriate questioning with students.
- ☐ Help students evaluate the merits of their questions.
- ☐ Qualify all comments, questions, compliments, and criticism.
- ☐ Encourage candor, humor, ingenuity, originality, and spontaneity.
- ☐ Follow process writing standards.
- ☐ Refrain from mailing letters with red-ink corrections.
- ☐ Mail only original letters—no form letters or dictation.
- ☐ Do not set deadlines for author responses.
- ☐ Do not send a guilt trip in order to encourage a response.
- ☐ Enclose #10 business size SASEs (self-addressed stamped envelopes).
- ☐ Verify legibility of return addresses on letters and SASEs.
- ☐ Make portfolio copies of letters, then mail them promptly.
- ☐ Encourage students to record the event in their journals.
- ☐ Wait patiently for a response.
- ☐ Photocopy single responses for the whole class.
- ☐ Allow students to share their letters and responses with the class.
- ☐ Conduct follow-up activities.

Write-the-Author Project Record

Student Name	Author Written	Date Mailed	Date Answered
		/ /	/ /
		/ /	/ /
		/ /	/ /
		/ /	/ /
		/ /	/ /
		/ /	/ /
		/ /	/ /
		/ /	/ /
		/ /	/ /
		/ /	/ /
		/ /	/ /
		/ /	/ /
		/ /	/ /
		/ /	/ /
		/ /	/ /
		/ /	/ /
		/ /	/ /
		/ /	/ /
		/ /	/ /
		/ /	/ /
		/ /	/ /
		/ /	/ /
		/ /	/ /
		/ /	/ /
		/ /	/ /
		/ /	/ /
		/ /	/ /
		/ /	/ /
		/ /	/ /
		/ /	/ /

Letter Writing Checklist for Children

☐ Have I chosen the author I'm writing?

☐ Have I read at least one book by the author I'm writing?

☐ Have I told about myself briefly?

☐ Have I mentioned and underlined the title of the book(s) I read?

☐ Have I given a comment about the book(s)?

☐ Have I asked a few specific meaningful questions?

☐ Do my questions and comments honestly reflect my thoughts?

☐ Have I asked for advice?

☐ Have I asked for a reply?

☐ Is my handwriting easy to read?

☐ Have I used friendly letter format?

☐ Have I enclosed a SASE (self-addressed stamped envelope)?

☐ Did I include a photo?

☐ Have I used correct envelope format?

Resources for Conducting Author Studies

Reference Books

Author Biographies Master Index. Gale Research, n.d.

Authors and Artists for Young Adults. Gale Research, n.d.

Biographies Master Index. Gale Research, n.d.

Children's Authors and Illustrators: An Index to Biographical Dictionaries. 5th Edition. Gale Research, 1995.

Contemporary Authors® Bibliographical Series. Gale Research, n.d.

Contemporary Authors®. Gale Research, n.d.

Contemporary Authors® Autobiography Series. Gale Research, n.d.

Contemporary Authors® Permanent Series. Gale Research, n.d.

Contemporary Popular Writers. Gale Research, 1997.

Dictionary of Literary Biography. Gale Research, n.d.

Directory of Illustrators, 8th edition. Morrow, 1992.

Hipple, Ted, ed. *Writers for Young Adults (3 volumes).* Scribners Reference, 1997.

Holtze, Sally Holmes. *Seventh Book of Junior Authors & Illustrators.* H. W. Wilson, 1996.

Kirkpatrick, D. L., ed. *Twentieth Century Children's Writers, 2nd edition.* St. Martins, 1983.

Laughlin, Jeannine L., and Sherry Laughlin. *Children's Authors Speak.* Libraries Unlimited, 1993.

Loertscher, David V., and Lance Castle. *A State-By-State Guide to Children's and Young Adult Authors and Illustrators.* Libraries Unlimited, 1991.

Loertscher, David V. *Biographical Index to Children's and Young Adult Authors and Illustrators.* Libraries Unlimited, 1991.

Major 20th-Century Writers. Gale Research, n.d.

Major Authors and Illustrators for Children and Young Adults: A Selection of Sketches from Something about the Author. Gale Research, 1993.

Roginski, Jim. *Behind the Covers: Interviews with Authors and Illustrators of Books for Children and Young Adults.* Vol. I and II. Libraries Unlimited, 1989.

Rollock, Barbara. *Black Authors and Illustrators of Children's Books.* Garland, 1992.

Silvey, Anita, ed. *Children's Books and Their Creators.* Houghton Mifflin, 1995.

Something about the Author. Gale Research, 1971-.

Something about the Author Autobiography Series. Gale Research, 1986-.

The Newbery and Caldecott Awards: A Guide to the Medal and Honor Books. American Library Association, 1998.

The Writer's Directory, 1998-2000. 13th edition. St. James/Gale Research, 1997.

Twentieth-Century Children'sWriters. 4th edition. St. James/Gale Research, 1994.

Twentieth-Century Young Adult Writers. St. James/Gale Research, 1994.

Wildberger, Mary Elizabeth. *Approaches to Literature through Authors.* Vol. 2 of *The Oryx Reading Motivation Series.* Oryx Press, 1993.

Professional Books

Allman, Barbara, and Marsha Jurca, eds. *Children's Authors and Illustrators*. Vol. 1. Frank Schaffer, 1991.

Allman, Barbara, Marsha Jurca, and Peggy Haynes, eds. *Children's Authors and Illustrators*. Vol. 2. Frank Schaffer, 1992.

_____. *Children's Authors and Illustrators*. Vol. 3. Frank Schaffer, 1992.

Blount, Jr., R. Howard, and Martha Venning Webb. *Art Projects Plus: Introducing Art Form, Media, and Technique with Children's Picture Books*. Instructional Fair • TS Denison, 1997.

Byrd, Kimberly S. *Jan Brett*. Teacher Created Materials, 1995.

Carratello, John, and Patty Carratello. *Eric Carle*. Teacher Created Materials, 1991.

Carratello, Patty. *Dr. Seuss*. Teacher Created Materials, 1991.

Cary, Alice. *Katherine Paterson*. The Learning Works, 1997.

Drew, Bernard A. *100 Most Popular Young Adult Authors: Biographical Sketches and Bibliographies*. Libraries Unlimited, 1997.

Gertridge, Allison. *Meet Canadian Authors and Illustrators: 50 Creators of Children's Books*. Scholastic Canada Ltd., 1994.

Hackett, Christine Olivieri. *Little House in the Classroom*. Good Apple, 1989.

Holzschuer, Cynthia. *Donald Crews/Ann Jonas*. Teacher Created Materials, 1996.

_____. *Gail Gibbons*. Teacher Created Materials, 1995.

_____. *James Marshall*. Teacher Created Materials, 1998.

Kelly, Joanne. *The Beverly Cleary Handbook*. Teacher Ideas, 1996.

Kotch, Laura, and Leslie Zackman. *The Author Studies Handbook: Helping Students Build Powerful Connections to Literature*. Scholastic, 1995.

Kovacs, Deborah. *Meet the Authors: 25 Writers of Upper Elementary and Middle School Books Talk About Their Work*. Scholastic, 1995.

Kovacs, Deborah, and James Preller. *Meet the Authors and Illustrators*. Scholastic, 1991.

_____. *Meet the Authors and Illustrators*. Volume Two. Scholastic, 1993.

Markham, Lois. *Lois Lowry*. The Learning Works, 1995.

McElmeel, Sharron L. *100 Most Popular Children's Authors: Biographical Sketches and Bibliographies*. Libraries Unlimited, 1998.

_____. *100 Most Popular Picture Book Authors and Illustrators: Biographical Sketches and Bibliographies*. Libraries Unlimited, 1999.

_____. *An Author a Month (for Nickels)*. Libraries Unlimited, 1990.

_____. *An Author a Month (for Pennies)*. Libraries Unlimited, 1988.

_____. *Authors for Children: A Calendar*. Libraries Unlimited, 1992.

_____. *Bookpeople: A First Album*. Libraries Unlimited, 1990.

_____. *Bookpeople: A Multicultural Album*. Libraries Unlimited, 1992.

_____. *Bookpeople: A Second Album*. Libraries Unlimited, 1990.

Nakajima, Caroline. *Roald Dahl*. Teacher Created Materials, 1996.

Norby, Shirley. *Famous Children's Authors*. T.S. Denison, 1988.

_____. *Famous Children's Authors, Book II*. T.S. Denison, 1989.

Norby, Shirley, and Gregory Ryan. *Famous Illustrators of Children's Literature*. T.S. Denison, 1990.

Onion, Susan. *Beverly Cleary*. Teacher Created Materials, 1996.

Palumbo, Thomas J. *Integrating the Literature of Beverly Cleary in the Classroom*. Good Apple, 1996.

_____. *Integrating the Literature of Chris Van Allsburg in the Classroom*. Good Apple, 1996.

_____. *Integrating the Literature of John Bellairs in the Classroom*. Good Apple, 1996.

▲▼▲

_____. *Integrating the Literature of Judy Blume in the Classroom.* Good Apple, 1996.

_____. *Integrating the Literature of Maurice Sendak in the Classroom.* Good Apple, 1993.

_____. *Integrating the Literature of Roald Dahl in the Classroom.* Good Apple, 1996.

Pecuch, Patricia. *Ezra Jack Keats.* Teacher Created Materials, 1997.

Puckett, Kathryn E., and Sara Laughlin, eds. *Directory of Indiana Children's Authors and Illustrators.* Stone Hills Area Library Services Authority, 1991.

Rice, Dona H. *Laura Ingalls Wilder.* Teacher Created Materials, 1998.

Rozakis, Laurie. *Meet the Author.* Troll, 1992.

Wyatt, Flora R., Margaret Coggins, and Jan Hunter Imber. *Popular Nonfiction Authors for Children: A Biographical and Thematic Guide.* Libraries Unlimited, 1998.

Books for Children

Aardema, Verna. *A Bookworm Who Hatched.* Richard C. Owen, 1992.

Adoff, Arnold. *Black Is Brown Is Tan.* Harper & Row, 1973.

Allen, Thomas B. *On Grandaddy's Farm.* Knopf, 1989.

Anderson, Gretchen, ed. *The Louisa May Alcott Cookbook.* Little Brown, 1985.

Andronik, Catherine M. *Kindred Spirit: A Biography of L. M. Montgomery, Creator of Anne of Green Gables.* Atheneum, 1993.

Asch, Frank. *One Man Show.* Richard C. Owen, 1997.

Ashabranner, Brent. *The Times of My Life: A Memoir.* Dutton, 1990.

Bauer, Marion Dane. *A Writer's Story: From Life to Fiction.* Clarion, 1995.

Becker, R. Margot. *Ann M. Martin: The Story of the Author of the Baby-Sitters Club.* Scholastic, 1993.

Berg, Julie. *Beverly Cleary.* Abdo & Daughters, 1993.

_____. *H. A. Rey.* Abdo & Daughters, 1994.

_____. *John Steptoe.* Abdo & Daughters, 1994.

_____. *Maurice Sendak.* Abdo & Daughters, 1993.

_____. *Richard Scarry.* Abdo & Daughters, 1994.

_____. *Tomie dePaola.* Abdo & Daughters, 1993.

Berg, Ken. *Maud Hart Lovelace.* Abdo & Daughters, 1994.

Bishop, Rudine Sims. *Presenting Walter Dean Myers.* Twayne, 1991.

Bloom, Susan P. *Presenting Avi.* Twayne, 1997.

Bloom, Susan P., and Cathryn M. Mercier. *Presenting Zibby O'Neal.* Twayne, 1991.

Blos, Joan W. *The Days Before Now: An Autobiographical Note by Margaret Wise Brown.* Simon & Schuster, 1994.

Boston, Lucy M. *Perverse and Foolish: A Memoir of Childhood and Youth.* Atheneum, 1979.

Bruce, Harry. *Maud: The Life of L. M. Montgomery.* Seal Bantam, 1992.

Bruchac, Joseph. *Bowman's Store: A Journey to Myself.* Dial, 1997.

_____. *Tell Me a Tale: A Book about Storytelling.* Harcourt Brace, 1997.

Bunting, Eve. *Once Upon a Time.* Richard C. Owen, 1995.

Byars, Betsy. *The Moon and I.* Julian Messner, 1991.

Campbell, Patricia J. *Presenting Robert Cormier.* Twayne, 1989.

Capote, Truman. *A Christmas Memory.* Knopf, 1989.

_____. *One Christmas.* Random House, 1983.

_____. *The Thanksgiving Visitor.* Knopf, 1996.

Carle, Eric. *The Art of Eric Carle.* Philomel, 1996.

_____. *Flora and Tiger: 19 Very Short Stories from My Life.* Putnam, 1997.

Carpenter, Angelica Shirley, and Jean Shirley. *Frances Hodgson Burnett: Beyond the Secret Garden.* Lerner, 1990.

_____. *L. Frank Baum: Royal Historian of Oz.* Lerner, 1992.

_____. *Robert Louis Stevenson: Finding Treasure Island.* Lerner, 1997.

Cart, Michael. *Presenting Robert Lipsyte.* Twayne, 1995.

Chaston, Joel D. *Lois Lowry.* Macmillan, 1997.

Christelow, Eileen. *What Do Authors Do?* Clarion, 1995.

Cleary, Beverly. *A Girl from Yamhill: A Memoir.* Morrow, 1988.

Cleary, Beverly. *My Own Two Feet: A Memoir.* Morrow, 1995.

Coatsworth, Elizabeth. *Personal Geography: Almost an Autobiography.* Stephen Greene Press, 1976.

Cole, Joanna, and Wendy Saul. *On the Bus with Joanna Cole: A Creative Autobiography.* Heinemann, 1996.

Collins, David R. *J. R. R. Tolkien: Master of Fantasy.* Lerner, 1992.

Cox, Clinton. *Mark Twain: America's Humorist, Dreamer, Prophet.* Scholastic, 1995.

Crews, Donald. *Bigmama's.* Greenwillow, 1991.

_____. *Shortcut.* Greenwillow, 1992.

Cummings, Pat. *Talking with Artists.* Bradbury, 1992.

_____. *Talking with Artists.* Vol. 2. Simon & Schuster, 1995.

_____. *Talking with Artists.* Vol. 3. Clarion, 1999.

Dahl, Roald. *BOY: Tales of Childhood.* Farrar, Straus & Giroux, 1984.

_____. *Going Solo: Continuing the Story Begun in BOY.* Farrar, Straus & Giroux, 1986.

Daly, John. *Presenting S.E. Hinton.* Twayne, 1989.

Davis, James E. *Presenting William Sleator.* Twayne, 1992.

Davis, Terry. *Presenting Chris Crutcher.* Twayne, 1997.

dePaola, Tomie. *The Art Lesson.* Putnam, 1989.

_____. *Twenty-Six Fairmont Avenue.* Putnam, 1999.

Dorsett, Lyle W., and Marjorie Lamp Mead, eds. *C. S. Lewis: Letters to Children.* Macmillan, 1985.

Duncan, Lois. *Chapters: My Growth as a Writer.* Little Brown, 1982.

Dyer, Daniel. *Jack London: A Biography.* Scholastic, 1997.

Ehlert, Lois. *Hands.* Harcourt Brace, 1997.

_____. *Under My Nose.* Richard C. Owen, 1996.

Ehrlich, Amy, ed. *When I Was Your Age: Original Stories about Growing Up.* Candlewick, 1996.

Emberley, Ed, Michael Emberley, and Rebecca Emberley. *Three: An Emberley Family Scrapbook.* Little Brown, 1998.

Engel, Dean, and Florence B. Freedman. *Ezra Jack Keats: A Biography with Illustrations.* Silver Moon Press, 1995.

Fleischman, Sid. *The Abracadabra Kid: A Writer's Life.* Greenwillow, 1996.

Foreman, Michael. *After the War Was Over: A Boy's Own Story.* Arcade, 1996.

_____. *War Boy: A Country Childhood.* Arcade, 1989.

Forman, Jack Jacob. *Presenting Paul Zindel.* Twayne, 1988.

Fox, Mem. *Memories: An Autobiography.* McDougal, Littell, 1992.

Fritz, Jean. *China Homecoming.* Putnam, 1985.

_____. *Harriet Beecher Stowe and the Beecher Preachers.* Putnam, 1994.

_____. *Homesick: My Own Story.* Putnam, 1982.

_____. *Surprising Myself.* Richard C. Owen, 1992.

Gallo, Don. *Presenting Richard Peck.* Twayne, 1989.

Gantos, Jack. *Heads or Tails: Stories from the Sixth Grade.* Farrar, Straus & Giroux, 1994.

Gantos, Jack. *Jack's Black Book*. Farrar, Straus & Giroux, 1997.

_____. *Jack's New Power: Stories from a Caribbean Year*. Farrar, Straus & Giroux, 1995.

Gardella, Tricia. *Writers in the Kitchen*. Boyds Mills, 1998.

Gherman, Beverly. *E. B. White: Some Writer!* Atheneum, 1992.

_____. *Robert Louis Stevenson: Teller of Tales*. Atheneum, 1996.

Goble, Paul. *Hau Kola Hello Friend*. Richard C. Owen, 1994.

Gormley, Beatrice. *C. S. Lewis: Christian and Storyteller*. Eerdmans, 1998.

Gonzales, Doreen. *Madeleine L'Engle: Author of "A Wrinkle in Time."* Dillon, 1991.

Greene, Carol. *Louisa May Alcott: Author, Nurse, Suffragette*. Childrens Press, 1984.

Greenfield, Eloise and Lessie Jones Little. *Childtimes: A Three-Generation Memoir*. Harper, 1979.

Harness, Cheryl. *Mark Twain and the Queens of the Mississippi*. Simon & Schuster, 1998.

Heller, Ruth. *Fine Lines*. Richard C. Owen, 1996.

Henry, Marguerite. *Dear Readers and Riders*. Rand McNally, 1969.

Hettinga, Donald R. *Presenting Madeleine L'Engle*. Twayne, 1993.

Hipple, Ted. *Presenting Sue Ellen Bridgers*. Twayne, 1990.

Holtze, Sally Holmes. *Presenting Norma Fox Mazer*. Twayne, 1987.

Hooper, Walter, ed. *Boxen: The Imaginary World of the Young C. S. Lewis*. Harcourt Brace, 1985.

Hopkins, Lee Bennett. *Been to Yesterdays: Poems of a Life*. Wordsong/Boyds Mills, 1995.

_____. *The Writing Bug*. Richard C. Owen, 1993.

Houston, Gloria. *My Great-Aunt Arizona*. HarperCollins, 1992.

Howe, James. *Playing with Words*. Richard C. Owen, 1994.

Hoyle, Karen Nelson. *Wanda Gag*. Twayne, 1994.

Hurwitz, Johanna. *A Dream Come True*. Richard C. Owen, 1998.

_____. *Astrid Lindgren: Storyteller to the World*. Viking Kestral, 1989.

Hyman, Trina Schart. *Self-Portrait: Trina Schart Hyman*. Addison-Wesley, 1981.

Johnson, Jane. *My Dear Noel: The Story of a Letter from Beatrix Potter*. Dial, 1999.

Johnson-Feelings, Dianne. *Presenting Laurence Yep*. Twayne, 1995.

Johnston, Norma. *Louisa May: The World and Works of Louisa May Alcott*. Four Winds Press, 1991.

Joyce, William. *The World of William Joyce*. HarperCollins, 1997.

Kehoe, Michael. *A Book Takes Root: The Making of a Picture Book*. Carolrhoda, 1993.

Kerr, M. E. *ME ME ME ME ME: Not a Novel*. Harper, 1983.

Kies, Cosette. *Presenting Lois Duncan*. Twayne, 1994.

Krull, Kathleen. *Lives of the Writers: Comedies, Tragedies (and What the Neighbors Thought)*. Harcourt Brace, 1994.

_____. *Presenting Paula Danziger*. Twayne, 1995.

Kuskin, Karla. *Thoughts, Pictures, and Words*. Richard C. Owen, 1995.

Lasky, Kathryn. *A Brilliant Streak: The Making of Mark Twain*. Harcourt Brace, 1998.

Lester, Helen. *Author: A True Story*. Houghton Mifflin, 1997.

Lewis, C. S., and Walter Hooper, ed. *On Stories: And Other Essays on Literature*. Harcourt Brace, 1982.

Little, Jean. *Little by Little: A Writer's Education*. Viking, 1988.

_____. *Stars Come Out Within*. Viking, 1991.

London, Jonathan. *Tell Me a Story*. Richard C. Owen, 1998.

Lowry, Lois. *Looking Back*. Houghton Mifflin, 1998.

Lyon, George Ella. *A Wordful Child*. Richard C. Owen, 1996.

Lyons, Mary E. *Keeping Secrets: The Girlhood Diaries of Seven Women Writers*. Holt, 1995.

Lee, Betsy. *Judy Blume's Story*. Macmillan, 1981.

Lewin, Ted. *I Was a Teenage Professional Wrestler*. Orchard, 1993.

MacDonald, Ruth K. *Dr. Seuss*. Twayne, 1988.

Mahy, Margaret. *My Mysterious World*. Richard C. Owen, 1995.

Marcus, Leonard S. *Margaret Wise Brown: Awakened by the Moon*. Beacon, 1992.

Martin, Patricia Stone. *Beverly Cleary: She Makes Reading Fun*. Reaching Your Goal Series. Rourke Enterprises, 1987.

Martin, Rafe. *A Storyteller's Story*. Richard Owen, 1992.

McKissack, Patricia. *Can You Imagine?* Richard C. Owen, 1997.

McPhail, David. *In Flight with David McPhail: A Creative Autobiography*. Heinemann, 1996.

Mee, Suzi. *Stories of the Poets*. Scholastic, 1990.

Meigs, Cornelia. *Invincible Louisa*. Little Brown, 1933.

Meltzer, Milton. *Starting from Home: A Writer's Beginnings*. Viking, 1988.

Miller, William. *Zora Hurston & the Chinaberry Tree*. Lee & Low, 1996.

Monseau, Virginia R. *Presenting Ouida Sebestyen*. Twayne, 1994.

Naylor, Phyllis Reynolds. *How I Came to Be a Writer*. Scholastic, 1987.

Neimark, Anne E. *Myth Maker: J. R. R. Tolkien*. Harcourt Brace, 1996.

Nesbit, E. *Long Ago When I Was Young*. Dial, 1987.

Nilsen, Alleen Pace. *Presenting M. E. Kerr*. Twayne, 1986.

Norris, Jerrie. *Presenting Rosa Guy*. Twayne, 1988.

Parks, Gordon. *Half Past Autumn: A Retrospective*. Little Brown, 1997.

Paulsen, Gary. *My Life in Dog Years*. Delacorte, 1998.

_____. *Puppies, Dogs, and Blue Northers: Reflections on Being Raised By a Pack of Sled Dogs*. Harcourt Brace, 1996.

_____. *Woodsong*. Bradbury, 1990.

Peck, Richard. *Anonymously Yours: A Memoir by the Author of Ghosts I Have Been*. Julian Messner, 1991.

Peet, Bill. *Bill Peet: An Autobiography*. Houghton Mifflin, 1989.

Pflieger, Pat. *Beverly Cleary*. Twayne, 1991.

Phy, Allene Stuart. *Presenting Norma Klein*. Twayne, 1988.

Pinkwater, Daniel. *Author's Day*. Macmillan, 1993.

Poe, Elizabeth Ann. *Presenting Barbara Wersba*. Twayne, 1998.

Polacco, Patricia. *Firetalking*. Richard C. Owen, 1994.

_____. *Meteor!* Dodd, Mead, 1987.

_____. *Mrs. Mack*. Philomel, 1998.

_____. *My Ol' Man*. Philomel, 1995.

_____. *My Rotten Redheaded Older Brother*. Simon & Schuster, 1994.

_____. *Some Birthday!* Simon & Schuster, 1991.

_____. *Thank You, Mr. Falker*. Philomel, 1998.

_____. *The Keeping Quilt*. Simon & Schuster, 1988.

_____. *The Trees of the Dancing Goats*. Simon & Schuster, 1996.

_____. *Thundercake*. Philomel, 1990.

Potter, Beatrix. *Letters to Children*. Walker, 1966.

Pringle, Laurence. *Nature! Wild and Wonderful*. Richard C. Owen, 1997.

Reed, Arthea J. S. *Presenting Harry Mazer*. Twayne, 1996.

Reef, Catherine. *John Steinbeck*. Clarion, 1996.

Reid, Suzanne Elizabeth. *Presenting Cynthia Voigt*. Twayne, 1995.

_____. *Presenting Ursula K. LeGuin*. Twayne, 1997.

Retan, Walter. *The Busy, Busy World of Richard Scarry*. Abrams, 1997.

Ringgold, Faith. *We Flew Over the Bridge: The Memoirs of Faith Ringgold*. Little Brown, 1995.

Ringgold, Faith, and Linda Freeman and Nancy Roucher. *Talking to Faith Ringgold.* Crown, 1996.

Rosen, Michael J. *Purr . . . : Children's Book Illustrators Brag about Their Cats.* Harcourt Brace, 1996.

_____. *Speak! Children's Book Illustrators Brag about Their Dogs.* Harcourt Brace, 1993.

Rylant, Cynthia. *Best Wishes.* Richard Owen, 1992.

_____. *But I'll Be Back Again: An Album.* Orchard, 1989.

_____. *Waiting to Waltz, A Childhood: Poems.* Bradbury, 1984.

_____. *Margaret, Frank, and Andy: Three Writers' Stories.* Harcourt Brace, 1996.

Salvner, Gary M. *Presenting Gary Paulsen.* Twayne, 1996.

Say, Allen. *Grandfather's Journey.* Houghton Mifflin, 1993.

_____. *The Inn-Keeper's Apprentice.* Houghton Mifflin, 1994.

Schmidt, Gary. *Robert McClosky.* Twayne, 1990.

Shannon, George. *Presenting Arnold Lobel.* Twayne, 1989.

Sonheim, Amy. *Presenting Maurice Sendak.* Twayne, 1992.

Spinelli, Jerry. *In My Own Words: Jerry Spinelli.* Simon & Schuster, 1997.

_____. *Knots in My Yo-Yo String: The Autobiography of a Kid.* Knopf, 1998.

Stan, Susan. *Presenting Lynn Hall.* Twayne, 1996.

Stevens, Janet. *From Pictures to Words: A Book about Making a Book.* Holiday House, 1995.

Stevenson, James. *Don't You Know There's a War On.* Greenwillow, 1992.

_____. *Fun No Fun.* Greenwillow, 1994.

_____. *Higher On the Door.* Greenwillow, 1987.

_____. *I Meant to Tell You.* Greenwillow, 1996.

_____. *July.* Greenwillow, 1990.

_____. *When I Was Nine.* Greenwillow, 1986.

Stover, Lois Thomas. *Presenting Phyllis Reynolds Naylor.* Twayne, 1997.

Sutcliff, Rosemary. *Blue Remembered Hills: A Recollection.* Morrow, 1983.

Taylor, Judy. *Beatrix Potter: An Artist, Storyteller, and Country Woman.* Warne, 1987.

Tingum, Janice. *E. B. White: The Elements of a Writer.* Lerner, 1995.

Tolkien, J. R. R. *The Father Christmas Letters.* George Allen & Unwin, 1976.

_____. *Letters from Father Christmas.* Houghton Mifflin, 1995.

Tudor, Bethany. *Drawn from New England: Tasha Tudor.* Putnam, 1979.

Tudor, Tasha, and Carol Johnston Lueck. *Tasha Tudor's Cookbook: Recipes and Reminiscences from Corgi Cottage.* Little Brown, 1993.

Turner, Robyn Montana. *Faith Ringgold.* Little Brown, 1993.

Uchida, Yoshiko. *The Invisible Thread: An Autobiography.* Julian Messner, 1991.

Van Leeuwen, Jean. *Growing Ideas.* Richard C. Owen, 1998.

Wadsworth, Ginger. *Laura Ingalls Wilder: Storyteller of the Prairie.* Lerner, 1997.

Walker, Barbara M. *The Little House Cookbook: Frontier Foods from Laura Ingalls Wilder's Classic Stories.* HarperCollins, 1979.

Wallner, Alexandra. *An Alcott Family Christmas.* Holiday House, 1996.

_____. *Beatrix Potter.* Holiday House, 1995.

_____. *Laura Ingalls Wilder.* Holiday House, 1997.

Weekly Reader's Read Magazine, ed. *Dear Author: Students Write about the Books that Changed Their Lives.* Conari, 1995.

Weidt, Maryann N. *Oh, the Places He Went: A Story about Dr. Seuss - Theodore Seuss Geisel.* Lerner, 1994.

_____. *Presenting Judy Blume.* Twayne, 1989.

Wheeler, Jill. *Dr. Seuss.* Abdo & Daughters, 1992.

_____. *Judy Blume.* Abdo & Daughters, 1996.

▲▼▲

Wilder, Laura Ingalls. *The Laura Ingalls Wilder Country Cookbook*. HarperCollins, 1995.
Willard, Nancy. *Cracked Corn and Snow Ice Cream: A Family Almanac*. Harcourt Brace, 1997.
Yates, Elizabeth. *Spanning Time: A Diary Keeper Becomes a Writer*. Cobblestone, 1996.
Yep, Laurence. *In My Own Words: The Lost Garden*. Julian Messner, 1991.
Yolen, Jane. *A Letter from Phoenix Farm*. Richard Owen, 1992.
Zemach, Margot. *Self-Portrait: Margot Zemach*. Addison-Wesley, 1978.
Zindel, Paul. *The Pigman and Me*. HarperCollins, 1992.

Books for Teachers and Librarians

Alderson, Brian, and Ezra Jack Keats. *Ezra Jack Keats: Artist and Picture-Book Maker*. Pelican, 1994.
Angelou, Maya. *I Know Why the Caged Bird Sings*. Random House, 1970.
Barry, Wendy E., Margaret Anne Doody, and Mary E. Doody Jones, eds. *The Annotated Anne of Green Gables*. Oxford, 1997.
Bawden, Nina. *In My Own Time: Almost an Autobiography*. Clarion, 1994.
Bickley, R. Bruce. *Joel Chandler Harris*. University of Georgia Press, 1978.
Carpenter, Humphrey. *The Inklings: C. S. Lewis, J. R. R. Tolkien, Charles Williams, and Their Friends*. Houghton Mifflin, 1979.
Cerf, Bennett. *At Random: The Reminiscences of Bennett Cerf*. Random House. 1977.
Chase, Carole F. *Suncatcher: A Study of Madeleine L'Engle and Her Writing*. Innisfree, 1998.
Cooper, Susan. *Dreams and Wishes: Essays on Writing for Children*. McElderry, 1996.
Copeland, Jeffrey S. *Speaking of Poets: Interviews with Poets Who Write for Children and Young Adults*. NCTE, 1993.
Elledge, Scott. *E. B. White: A Biography*. Norton, 1984.
Elleman, Barbara, ed. *Books Change Lives: Quotes to Treasure*. Booklist, 1994.
Fensch, Thomas, ed. *Of Sneeches and Whos and the Good Dr. Seuss: Essays on the Writings and Life of Theodore Geisel*. McFarland, 1997.
Fox, Mem. *Dear Mem Fox, I Have Read All Your Books Even the Pathetic Ones*. Harcourt Brace, 1992.
_____. *Radical Reflections: Passionate Opinions on Teaching, Learning, and Living*. Harcourt Brace, 1993.
Gallo, Donald, ed. *Speaking for Ourselves, Too: More Author Biographical Sketches by Notable Authors of Books for Young Adults*. NCTE, 1992.
Gallo, Donald R. *Author's Insights: Turning Teenagers into Readers and Writers*. Heinemann, 1992.
Gardella, Tricia. *Writers in the Kitchen: Children's Book Authors Share Memories of Their Favorite Recipes*. Boyds Mills, 1998.
Gilbert, Douglas, and Clyde S. Kilby. *C. S. Lewis: Images of His World*. Eerdmans, 1973.
Guth, Dorothy L., ed. *The Letters of E. B. White*. Harper & Row, 1989.
Hopkins, Lee Bennett. *Pauses: Autobiographical Reflections of 101 Creators of Children's Books*. HarperCollins, 1995.
Konigsburg, E. L. *TalkTalk: A Children's Book Author Speaks to Grown-ups*. Simon & Schuster, 1995.
L'Engle, Madeleine. *A Circle of Quiet*. The Crosswicks Journal, Book One. HarperCollins, 1987.
_____. *The Irrational Season*. The Crosswicks Journal, Book Three. HarperCollins, 1979.
_____.*The Summer of the Great-Grandmother*. The Crosswicks Journal, Book Two. HarperCollins, 1996.
L'Engle, Madeleine. *Two-Part Invention: The Story of a Marriage*. The Crosswicks Journal, Book Four. HarperCollins, 1989.

▲▼▲

Lewis, C. S. *The Letters of C. S. Lewis*. Harcourt Brace, 1966.

_____. *Surprised By Joy*. Harcourt Brace, 1955.

Lindskoog, Kathryn. *The Lion of Judah in Never-Never Land: God, Man & Nature in C. S. Lewis's Narnia Tales*. Eerdmans, 1973.

Lionni, Leo. *Between Worlds: The Autobiography of Leo Lionni*. Knopf, 1997.

Lord, Graham. *James Herriot: The Life of a Country Vet*. Macmillan, 1998.

Marantz, Kenneth A., and Sylvia S. Marantz. *Artists of the Page: Interviews with Children's Book Illustrators*. McFarland, 1992.

Martin, Tovah and Richard Brown. *Tasha Tudor's Garden*. Houghton Mifflin, 1994.

_____. *Tasha Tudor's Heirloom Crafts*. Houghton Mifflin, 1995.

Meyer, Susan E. *A Treasury of the Great Children's Book Illustrators*. Abrams, 1997.

Moates, Marianne M. *A Bridge of Childhood: Truman Capote's Southern Years*. Holt, 1989.

Morgan, Judith, and Neil Morgan. *Dr. Seuss and Mr. Geisel: A Biography*. Da Capo Press, 1996.

Neumeyer, Peter F., ed. *The Annotated Charlotte's Web*. HarperCollins, 1994.

Nordstrom, Ursula, and Leonard S. Marcus, eds. *Dear Genius: The Letters of Ursula Nordstrom*. HarperCollins, 1998.

Paterson, Katherine. *Gates of Excellence: On Reading & Writing Books for Children*. Lodestar, 1981.

_____. *A Sense of Wonder: On Reading and Writing Books for Children* (Gates of Excellence and The Spying Heart in one volume). Plume, 1995.

_____. *The Spying Heart: More Thoughts on Reading and Writing Books for Children*. Lodestar, 1990.

Paulsen, Gary. *Eastern Sun, Winter Moon: An Autobiographical Odyssey*. Harcourt Brace, 1993.

Paulsen, Gary. *Winterdance: The Fine Madness of Running the Iditarod*. Harcourt Brace, 1994.

Peck, Robert Newton. *My Vermont*. Peck Press, 1985.

Pomerance, Murray. *Ludwig Bemelmans: A Comprehensive Bibliography*. Heineman, 1995.

Rees, David. *Painted Desert, Green Shade: Essays on Contemporary Writers for Children and Young Adults*. Horn Book, 1984.

Sayer, George. *Jack: A Life of C. S. Lewis*. Crossway Books, 1994.

Smith, Jane Stuart, and Betty Carlson. *Great Women Authors: Their Lives and Their Literature*. Crossway, 1999.

Taylor, Judy, ed. *Beatrix Potter's Letters*. Warne, 1989.

Trelease, Jim. *Hey! Listen to This: Stories to Read Aloud*. Penguin, 1992.

_____. *Read All About It! Great Read-Aloud Stories, Poems, and Newspaper Pieces for Preteens and Teens*. Penguin, 1993.

_____. *The New Read-Aloud Handbook*. Penguin, 1989.

Tudor, Tasha, and Richard Brown. *The Private World of Tasha Tudor*. Little Brown, 1992.

Willard, Nancy. *Telling Time: Angels, Ancestors, and Stories*. Harcourt Brace, 1993.

Wintle, Justin, *The Pied Pipers: Interview with the Influential Creators of Children's Literature*. Paddington Press, 1975.

Yunghens, Penelope. *Prize Winners: Ten Writers for Young Readers*. Morgan Reynolds, 1996.

▲▼▲

Interview Audio Tapes

Base, Graeme. Scholastic, 1994.
Brett, Jan. The Trumpet Club, 1992.
Bunting, Eve. The Trumpet Club, 1991.
Conrad, Pam. Scholastic, 1992.
Coville, Bruce. Scholastic, 1993.
Dadey, Debbie and Marcia Thornton Jones. Scholastic, 1996.
Dahl, Roald. The Trumpet Club, 1992.
dePaola, Tomie. The Trumpet Club, 1989.
Ehlert, Lois. The Trumpet Club,1993.
Freedman, Russell. Scholastic, 1991.
Fritz, Jean. The Trumpet Club, 1991.
Fox, Mem. The Trumpet Club, 1992.
Fox, Paula. The Trumpet Club, 1990.
Fox Paula. The Trumpet Club, 1993.
Hamilton, Virginia. Scholastic, 1992.
Hinton, S.E. The Trumpet Club, 1988.
Hopkins, Lee Bennett and Nikki Giovanni and X.J. Kennedy. The Trumpet Club, 1992.
Howe, James. The Trumpet Club, 1993.
Lauber, Patricia. Scholastic, 1992.
Lowry, Lois. The Trumpet Club, 1990.
Lowry, Lois. The Trumpet Club, 1994.
Kellogg, Steven. The Trumpet Club, 1989.
L'Engle, Madeleine. The Trumpet Club, 1990.
Little, Jean. The Trumpet Club, 1990.
Macaulay, David. Scholastic, 1992.
Macaulay, David. The Trumpet Club, 1989.
MacLachlan, Patricia. The Trumpet Club, 1992.
McDaniel, Lurlene. The Trumpet Club, 1992.
McKissack, Patricia. Scholastic, 1993.
Naylor, Phyllis Reynolds. The Trumpet Club, 1992.
Paulsen, Gary. The Trumpet Club, 1990.
Paulsen, Gary. The Trumpet Club, 1993.
Peck, Richard. The Trumpet Club, 1987.
Polacco, Patricia. The Trumpet Club, 1993.
Rylant, Cynthia. The Trumpet Club, 1993.
Myers, Walter Dean. Scholastic, 1993.
Paulsen, Gary. Scholastic, 1991.
Sachar, Louis. The Trumpet Club, 1990.
Say, *Allen.* Scholastic, 1992.
Scieska, Jon and Lane Smith. The Trumpet Club, 1993.
Soto, Gary. The Trumpet Club, 1992.
Speare, Elizabeth George. The Trumpet Club, 1990.
Spinelli, Jerry. Scholastic, 1991.
Taylor, Mildred. The Trumpet Club, 1990.
Taylor, Theodore. The Trumpet Club, 1987.

▲▼▲

Wiesner, David. Scholastic, 1992.

Williams, Vera B. The Trumpet Club, 1992.

Wright, Betty Ren. Scholastic, 1993.

On Becoming a Writer authortalks (Avi, Natalie Babbitt, Judy Blume, Paula Fox, Russell Freedman, Jamie Gilson, James Howe, Lois Lowry, Patricia McKissack, Seymour Simon). The Children's Book Council, 1992.

Videos

The Author's Eye: Roald Dahl. SRA/McGraw-Hill, 1988.

The Author's Eye: Katherine Paterson. SRA/McGraw-Hill, 1988.

Beatrix Potter Had a Pet Named Peter. SRA/McGraw-Hill, n.d.

Bill Peet in His Studio. Houghton Mifflin, 1982.

Celebrating Authors Video Series: Meet Carol Gorman. Libraries Unlimited, 1992.

Celebrating Authors Video Series: Meet Jacqueline Briggs Martin. Libraries Unlimited, 1992.

David Macaulay in His Studio. Houghton Mifflin, 1981.

Eric Carle: Picture Writer. Philomel, 1993.

Faith Ringgold: The Last Story Quilt. Public Media Home Vision, 1991.

Fiction and Other Truths: A Film About Jane Rule. Cinema Guild, 1995.

Get to Know Bernard Most. Harcourt Brace, 1993.

Get to Know Gerald McDermott. Harcourt Brace, 1996.

Get to Know Keith Baker. Harcourt Brace, 1994.

Get to Know Lynne Cherry. Harcourt Brace, 1993.

Get to Know Lois Ehlert. Harcourt Brace, 1994.

Getting to Know William Steig. Weston Woods, 1995.

Going Home with Gloria Houston. Ameriquest Enterprises, 1994.

Good Conversation! A Talk with Aliki. Tim Podell Productions, 1997.

Good Conversation! A Talk with Ann McGovern. Tim Podell Productions, 1991.

Good Conversation! A Talk with Avi. Tim Podell Productions, 1995.

Good Conversation! A Talk with Betsy Byars. Tim Podell Productions, 1994.

Good Conversation! A Talk with Bruce Coville. Tim Podell Productions, 1993.

Good Conversation! A Talk with Chaim Potok. Tim Podell Productions, 1997.

Good Conversation! A Talk with E. L. Konigsburg. Tim Podell Productions, 1995.

Good Conversation! A Talk with Jean Craighead George. Tim Podell Productions, 1991.

Good Conversation! A Talk with Jean Fritz. Tim Podell Productions, 1993.

Good Conversation! A Talk with Jerry Spinelli. Tim Podell Productions, 1994.

Good Conversation! A Talk with Joan Lowery Nixon. Tim Podell Productions, 1996.

Good Conversation! A Talk with Johanna Hurwitz. Tim Podell Productions, 1997.

Good Conversation! A Talk with Karen Hesse. Tim Podell Productions, 1998.

Good Conversation! A Talk with Karla Kuskin. Tim Podell Productions, 1991.

Good Conversation! A Talk with Laurence Yep. Tim Podell Productions, 1998.

Good Conversation! A Talk with Lee Bennett Hopkins. Tim Podell Productions, 1991.

Good Conversation! A Talk with Lurlene McDaniel. Tim Podell Productions, 1997.

Good Conversation! A Talk with Lynne Reid Banks. Tim Podell Productions, 1995.

Good Conversation! A Talk with M. E. Kerr. Tim Podell Productions, 1991.

Good Conversation! A Talk with Madeleine L'Engle. Tim Podell Productions, 1994.

Good Conversation! A Talk with Matt Christopher. Tim Podell Productions, 1994.

Good Conversation! A Talk with Nancy Willard. Tim Podell Productions, 1991.

Good Conversation! A Talk with Natalie Babbitt. Tim Podell Productions, 1995.

Good Conversation! A Talk with Patricia Reilly Giff. Tim Podell Productions, 1996.

Good Conversation! A Talk with Paula Fox. Tim Podell Productions, 1992.

Good Conversation! A Talk with Phyllis Reynolds Naylor. Tim Podell Productions, 1991.

Good Conversation! A Talk with Richard Peck. Tim Podell Productions, 1997.

Good Conversation! A Talk with Robert Cormier. Tim Podell Productions, 1996.

Good Conversation! A Talk with Robert Newton Peck. Tim Podell Productions, 1998.

Good Conversation! A Talk with Robin McKinley. Tim Podell Productions, 1997.

Good Conversation! A Talk with the McKissacks. Tim Podell Productions, 1997.

Good Conversation! A Talk with Theodore Taylor. Tim Podell Productions, 1998.

Good Conversation! A Talk with Zilpha Keatley Snyder. Tim Podell Productions, 1998.

James Marshall in His Studio. Houghton Mifflin, 1987.

Jean Fritz. Putnam, 1986.

Madeleine L'Engle: Star*Gazer. Ishtar Films, 1989.

The Making of a Storybook: Mary Calhoun—Storyteller. Chip Taylor Communications, 1991.

Maurice Sendak. Weston Woods, 1986.

Meet Ashley Bryan: Storyteller, Artist, Writer. SRA/McGraw-Hill, 1991.

Meet Jack Prelutsky. SRA/McGraw-Hill, 1991.

Meet Janet Taylor Lisle. SRA/McGraw-Hill, n.d.

Meet Leo Lionni. SRA/McGraw-Hill, 1992.

Meet Marc Brown. American School Publishers, 1991.

Meet Stan and Jan Berenstain. SRA/McGraw-Hill, 1991.

Meet the Author: A. A. Milne (and the Pooh). SRA/McGraw-Hill, n.d.

Meet the Author: Ashley Bryan and Jack Prelutsky (videodisc). SRA/McGraw-Hill, n.d.

Meet the Author: Cynthia Rylant (videodisc). SRA/McGraw-Hill, n.d.

Meet the Author: Gordon Korman. School Services of Canada, 1991.

Meet the Author: Hans Christian Andersen. SRA/McGraw-Hill, n.d.

Meet the Author: Henry Wadsworth Longfellow. SRA/McGraw-Hill, n.d.

Meet the Author: Jean Little—Mind's Eyecolor. School Services of Canada, 1996.

Meet the Author: Leo Lionni (videodisc). SRA/McGraw-Hill, n.d.

Meet the Author: Louisa May Alcott. SRA/McGraw-Hill, n.d.

Meet the Author: Mildred Taylor (videodisc). SRA/McGraw-Hill, n.d.

Meet the Author: Robert Louis Stevenson. SRA/McGraw-Hill, n.d.

Meet the Author/Illustrator: C.J. Taylor. School Services of Canada, 1994.

Meet the Caldecott Illustrator: Jerry Pinkney. SRA/McGraw-Hill, 1991.

Meet the Newbery Author: Arnold Lobel. SRA/McGraw-Hill, 1991.

Meet the Newbery Author: Betsy Byars. SRA/McGraw-Hill, n.d.

Meet the Newbery Author: Cynthia Rylant. SRA/McGraw-Hill, n.d.

Meet the Newbery Author: Eleanor Estes. SRA/McGraw-Hill, n.d.

Meet the Newbery Author: Jean Craighead George. SRA/McGraw-Hill, 1989.

Meet the Newbery Author: Laura Ingalls Wilder. SRA/McGraw-Hill, n.d.

Meet the Newbery Author: Madeleine L'Engle. SRA/McGraw-Hill, n.d.

Meet the Newbery Author: Marguerite Henry. SRA/McGraw-Hill, n.d.

Meet the Newbery Author: Mildred D. Taylor. SRA/McGraw-Hill, 1991.

Meet the Newbery Author: Russell Freedman. SRA/McGraw-Hill, 1991.

Meet the Newbery Author: Scott O'Dell. SRA/McGraw-Hill, n.d.

Meet the Newbery Author: Virginia Hamilton. SRA/McGraw-Hill, n.d.
Meet the Picture Book Author: Cynthia Rylant. SRA/McGraw-Hill, 1990.
Patricio Polacco: Dream Keeper. Philomel, 1996.
The Real, the True, the Gen-u-ine Wizard of Oz: L. Frank Baum. SRA/McGraw-Hill, n.d.
Take Joy! The Magical World of Tasha Tudor. Scholastic/Weston Woods, n.d.
Trumpet Video Visits: Donald Crews. The Trumpet Club, 1992.
Trumpet Video Visits: Mem Fox. The Trumpet Club, 1992.
Trumpet Video Visits: Steven Kellogg. The Trumpet Club, 1993.
Trumpet Video Visits: Katherine Paterson. The Trumpet Club, 1993.
Trumpet Video Visits: Gary Paulsen. The Trumpet Club, 1992.
A Visit with Barbara Cooney. Viking/Puffin, 1995.
A Visit with Eve Bunting. Clarion/Houghton Mifflin, 1991.
A Visit with Jean Craighead George. Penguin, n.d.
A Visit with Jean Fritz. Philomel, n.d.
A Visit with Jerry Pinkney. Dial/Puffin, 1995.
A Visit with Lloyd Alexander. Dutton/Penguin, 1994.
A Visit with Lois Lowry. Clarion/Houghton Mifflin, 1985.
A Visit with Paul O. Zelinsky. Dutton/Puffin, 1995.
A Visit with Rosemary Wells. Dial/Puffin, 1995.
A Visit with Russell Freedman. Clarion/Houghton Mifflin, 1990.
A Visit with Scott O'Dell. Houghton Mifflin, 1983.
A Visit with Tomie dePaola. Putnam, 1997.
Who's Dr. Seuss? Meet Ted Geisel. SRA/McGraw-Hill, n.d.

CD-ROMs

Contemporary Authors®. GaleNet, n.d.
Dictionary of Literary Biography Online. GaleNet, n.d.
DISCovering Authors®, 2.0. GaleNet, n.d.
Loertscher, David V. and Lance Castle. *A State-By-State Guide to Children's and Young Adult Authors and Illustrators.* Libraries Unlimited, 1991. (Apple, Mac, IBM)
Scribner Writers on CD-ROM, Release 2.0. Scribner Reference, n.d.
Twayne's English Authors on CD-ROM. Twayne, n.d.
Twayne's U. S. Authors on CD-ROM. Twayne, n.d.
Twayne's Women Authors on CD-ROM. Twayne, 1996.
Twayne's World Authors on CD-ROM. Twayne, n.d.
U•X•L Junior DISCovering Authors®, 2.0. GaleNet, 1998.

Author and Illustrator Resources on the Internet

The Author Guru's Children's Corner

http://www.geocities.com/Athens/Acropolis/4617/agkidspage.html

Author's Pen

http://www.books.com/scripts/authors.exe

Birthdates of Children's Authors

gopher://lib.nmsu.edu/11/.subjects/Education/.childlit/.authors/.birthdates

The Canadian Teacher-Librarians' Resource Pages

http://www.geocities.com/Athens/Olympus/1333/resource.htm

Children's Literature Authors & Illustrators

http://web.nwe.ufl.edu/~jbrown/chauth.html

Children's Literature Web Guide

http://www.acs.ucalgary.ca/~dkbrown/new.html

Children's Writing Resource Center

http://www.write4kids.com

The Drawing Board for Illustrators

members.aol.com/thedrawing/

Electronic Resources for Youth Services

http://www.chebucto.ns.ca/~aa331/childlit.html

Fairrosa Cyber Library/Authors & Illustrators

http://www.users.interport.net/~fairrosa/cl.authors.html

Harold Underdown's Purple Crayon

http://www.users.interport.net/~hdu

▲▼▲

Inkspot: The Writer's Resource

http://www.inkspot.com

Internet Public Library's Author Biographies

http://www.ipl.org/youth/AskAuthor/Biographies.html

Just For Kids Who Love Books

http://www.geocities.com/Athens/Olympus/1333/kids.htm

Mona Kerby's The Author Corner

http://www.carr.org/authco/

***Once Upon a Time* Magazine**

members.aol.com/ouatmag/index.html

An Outstanding Collection of Children's Authors

http://weber.u.washington.edu/~celes/ss96/_teach17.htm

The Scoop's Interviews of Authors and Illustrators

http://www.Friend.ly.Net/scoop/biographies/

USM de Grummond Children's Literature Collection

http://avatar.lib.usm.edu/~degrum/

Dr. Mary Ellen Van Camp
Once Upon a Time . . . A Children's Literature Site

http://nova.bsuvc.bsu.edu/~00mevancamp/index.html

Kay Vandergrift's Children's Literature Page

http://www.scils.rutgers.edu/special/kay/childlit.html

Yahooligans! Directory of Author Sites

http://www.yahooligans.com/Art_Soup/Books_and_Reading/authors

Children's Books Newsgroup

rec.arts.books.childrens

▲▼▲

Sources for Arranging
Author and Illustrator Visits

The following sources will be of assistance if you plan to schedule an author visit at your school, library, or conference. There is a certain protocol to follow if the visits are to be successful. Be sure to do your homework before attempting to schedule a literary event.

Publications

East, Kathy. *Inviting Children's Authors and Illustrator: A How-To-Do-It Manual for School and Public Librarians.* Neal-Schuman, 1995.

Inviting Children's Book Authors and Illustrators to Your Community. The Children's Book Council, 1992.

Melton, David. *How to Capture Live Authors and Bring Them to Your Schools.* Landmark Editions, 1986.

New England Authors and Illustrators of Children's Books. New England Booksellers Association, 1992.

Watkins, Jan. *Programming Author Visits.* ALA Editions, 1996.

Web Sites

Author Illustrator Source

Web Site: http://www.author-illustr-source.com

E-mail: poughton@aol.com

The Author Illustrator Source is a web site hosted by Paul Oughton, husband of children's author Jerrie Oughton. The web site features a national listing of children's authors and illustrators who travel for speaking engagements to schools, libraries, and conferences. Author and illustrator listings are organized both by geographical regions and by state to facilitate those looking for local authors. Individual author listings include the following features:

- a biographical sketch
- selected listing of published titles and graphics of book covers
- link to Amazon for book purchases
- types of presentations the authors and illustrators make
- number and length of presentation sessions made per visit, equipment/facility needs, professional fees, and travel expenses
- how to contact the author or representative by phone, e-mail, or snail mail
- links to authors' and illustrators' personal web pages.

Web Sites (Continued)

Invite An Author

http://www.snowcrest.net/kidpower/authors.html

Authors and Illustrators Who Visit Schools

http://www.teleport.com/~authilus/

Steven Michael Harris

Links to School Presentations Touring the Eastern United States

http://home.maine.rr.com/smharris/perfrms.htm

Jame Magdanz

Invite an Author to Your School

http://magdanz.com/books/river/authors.htm

The Children's Book Guild Speakers Bureau

http://www.childrensbookguild.org/SpeakersBureau.html

Children's Books with Letter Writing Themes

Bang, Molly. *Delphine*. Morrow, 1988.

Brandt, Betty. *Special Delivery*. Carolrhoda, 1988.

Brisson, Pat. *Kate on the Coast*. Bradbury, 1992.

_____. *Your Best Friend*. Bradbury, 1989.

Brown, Marc. *Arthur Goes to Camp*. Little Brown, 1982.

Bunin, Sherry. *Dear Great American Writers School*. Houghton Mifflin, 1995.

Campbell, Rod. *Dear Zoo*. Macmillan, 1982.

Caseley, Judith. *Dear Annie*. Greenwillow, 1991.

Cleary, Beverly. *Dear Mr. Henshaw*. Morrow, 1983.

Conford, Ellen. *Dear Lovey Hart: I Am Desperate*. Little Brown, 1975.

Cushman, Karen. *The Ballad of Lucy Whipple*. Clarion, 1996.

Dolphin, Laurie. *Georgia to Georgia*. Tambourine, 1991.

Dragonwagon, Crescent. *Dear Miss Moshki*. Macmillan, 1986.

Duffey, Betsy. *Utterly Yours, Booker Jones*. Viking, 1995.

Dupasquier, Philippe. *Dear Daddy*. Bradbury, 1985.

Gibbons, Gail. *The Post Office Book: Mail and How It Moves*. HarperCollins, 1982.

Giff, Patricia Reilly. *The War Began at Supper: Letters to Miss Loria*. Delacorte, 1991.

Goldberg, Sue. *Dear Bronx Zoo*. Macmillan, 1991.

Greene, Constance. *The Love Letters of J. Timothy Owen*. HarperCollins, 1986.

Greenwald, Sheila. *Mariah Delany's Author-of-the-Month Club*. Little Brown, 1990.

Hoban, Lillian. *Arthur's Pen Pal*. HarperCollins, 1976.

James, Simon. *Dear Mr. Blueberry*. Macmillan/Margaret K. McElderry, 1991.

Keats, Ezra Jack. *A Letter to Amy*. HarperCollins, 1968.

Leedy, Loreen. *Messages in the Mailbox: How to Write a Letter*. Holiday House, 1991.

MacLachlan, Patricia. *Sarah, Plain and Tall*. HarperCollins, 1985.

Marshak, Samuel. *Hail to the Mail*. Holt, 1990.

Mazer, Norma Fox. *After the Rain*. Morrow, 1987.

_____. *Dear Bill, Remember Me?* Dell, 1976.

_____. *Taking Terri Mueller*. Avon, 1981.

Miles, Betty. *Save the Earth!* Knopf, 1991.

Mischel, Florence. *How to Write a Letter*. Watts, 1988.

Moore, Inga. *Little Dog Lost*. Macmillan, 1991.

Parker, Nancy Winslow. *Love from Aunt Betty*. Putnam, 1983.

Parks, Rosa, and Gregory J. Reed. *Dear Mrs. Parks: A Dialogue with Today's Youth*. Lee & Low, 1996.

Pfeffer, Susan. *Dear Dad, Love Laurie*. Scholastic, 1989.

Potter, Beatrix. *Dear Peter Rabbit: A Story with Real Miniature Letters*. Warne, 1995.

Richardson, Arleta. *Letters from Grandma's Attic*. Chariot, 1995.

Roth, Harold. *First Class! The Postal System in Action*. Pantheon, 1983.

Sampton, Sheila. *Jenny's Journey*. Viking, 1991.

Sanford, Doris. *Love Letters: Responding to Children in Pain*. Multnomah, 1991.

Silverberg, Robert. *Letters from Atlantis*. Atheneum, 1990.

Smith, Samantha. *Samantha Smith: Journey to the Soviet Union*. Little Brown, 1985.

▲▼▲

Turner, Ann. *Nettie's Trip South*. Macmillan, 1987.
Uchida, Yoshiko. "Letter from a Concentration Camp." *The Big Book for Peace*. Dutton, 1990.
Williams, Vera B. *Stringbean's Trip to the Shining Sea*. Greenwillow, 1988.
Wilson, Cara. *Love, Otto: The Legacy of Anne Frank*. Andrews and McMeel, 1995.
Winnick, Karen B. *Mr. Lincoln's Whiskers*. Boyds Mills, 1996.
Zimelman, Nathan. *Please Excuse Jasper*. Abingdon, 1987.

Book Club Addresses

Scholastic Book Clubs
P.O. Box 7503
Jefferson City, MO 65102-7503
(800) 724-6527

Trumpet Book Clubs
P.O. Box 7510
Jefferson City, MO 65102-7510
(800) 826-0110

Troll Book Clubs
2 Lethbridge Plaza
Mahwah, NJ 07430-9986
(800) 541-1097

Carnival Book Clubs
P.O. Box 3730
Jefferson City, MO 65102-3730
(800) 654-3037

R. Howard Blount, Jr.

Author

▲▼

Born: October 3, 1958
Address: 603 W. Dixie St.
Plant City, FL 33566
E-mail: bullet1234@aol.com
Web Site: http://www.author-illustr-source.
com/ais_4fl.htm#blount

Selected Titles

1999 - The Address Book of Children's Authors
and Illustrators, 2nd edition
1997 - Language Arts Lingo: Glossaries
and Flashcards for 200+ Terms
1997 - Art Projects Plus: Introducing Art
Form, Media, and Technique
with Children's Picture Books
1996 - Implementing Literature-Based
Instruction and Authentic Assessment
1994 - The Address Book of Children's Authors
and Illustrators
1994 - Linking Reading Assessment to
Instruction (contributor)

Howard Blount loves to hear responses from teachers, librarians, children, and others who have used his books.

R. Howard Blount Jr. was born a fourth generation Floridian in Tampa, Florida, but when he was 11 years old, his parents became missionaries to Latin America. The Blount family lived in the countries of Mexico, Chile, and Paraguay, where young "Howie" grew up speaking Spanish as a second language.

Many years later, in 1980, Mr. Blount began his career as a classroom teacher with Hillsborough County Schools in Florida. He earned a B.A. in elementary education from Southeastern College and an M.Ed. in educational leadership from the University of South Florida. Over the years Howard wrote numerous theme units, designed a system of portfolio assessment, conducted workshops, wrote for district committees, and was named a Florida Associate Master Teacher. Mr. Blount's fascination with corresponding with authors led to the publication of his first book, *The Address Book of Children's Authors and Illustrators*, which now in its second edition has become his newest book.

Howard enjoys reading, singing and songwriting, playing with Aubrey and Taylor, his miniature long-haired dachshunds, collecting first editions, playing his extensive CD collection, and listening to Joyce Meyer and T. D. Jakes teaching tapes.

▲▼▲

I'd Like to Hear From You . . .

If you are a teacher, librarian, or student who has found this resource to be useful and you have a success story to share, I would enjoy hearing from you. If there are authors you would like to see included in future editions, please send me the information you have, including the authors' addresses if possible, so that I may contact them. Should you have ideas to further facilitate the correspondence process or ideas for activities to contribute, full credit will be given when the ideas are used with subsequent publication. And of course feedback of any kind is always welcomed. Remember to send all correspondence with a SASE.

Published authors and illustrators who desire a listing in future editions, please write me for an information packet. Your evaluative responses are also greatly appreciated.

I am available for speaking engagements at schools, libraries, workshops, and conferences on the topics of corresponding with authors, literature-based instruction, authentic assessment, and how teachers and librarians can get their ideas published. Please visit my web site for more information.

Address: R. Howard Blount, Jr.
603 W. Dixie St.
Plant City, FL 33566
(813) 752-4131

E-mail: bullet1234@aol.com
Web Site: http://www.author-illustr-source.com/ais_4fl.htm#blount

Acknowledgments

My infinite appreciation to:

- my 1992–93 and 1993–94 sixth grade language arts students at Lincoln Elementary, Plant City, Florida, who chose to write authors and illustrators, let me enjoy their responses vicariously, stuffed, sealed, and stamped envelopes, listened to my endless excited chatter about "the book," and hopefully learned a lot about literature in the process

- all of the authors and illustrators who cared enough to respond

- Martha Webb, Becky Brewer, Jason Greenway, and Molly Sapp who assisted me with proofing the first draft manuscript

- Barbara Elleman—who kindly responded to my inquiries and requests

- Joan Lowery Nixon—who laid it on the line in black and white

- Johanna Hurwitz and Norma Fox Mazer—two givers and true believers

- Gloria Houston—not only an author whose work I highly admire, but one of my all-time favorite people. Gloria was the first author to give me encouragement with the possibilities of this book and to direct me to conduct preliminary research. She has openly and candidly shared with me her experiences—poignant family scenes from her Appalachian background; drafts and subsequent stages from her published work; engaging conversation over Italian food or a bowl of soup; and networking to promote my work among people in the business of books. One of the highlights from my teaching career was being able to share and allow my students to critique a preliminary draft of Ms. Houston's *Mountain Valor*. I am truly blessed.

2nd Edition

- barnesandnoble@aol and amazon.com for assistance with copyright dates and titles

- Debra Olson Pressnall—my wonderful editor at Instructional Fair • TS Denison for graciously accomodating my temperamental nature on the last three books

- Diane Vanderkooy at Scholastic Canada, Ltd. for her assistance on the last two books

Sources

Books

Books in Print 1993-94. R. R. Bowker, 1993.

Cleary, Beverly. *Dear Mr. Henshaw*. Morrow, 1983.

Cummings, Pat. *Talking with Artists*. Bradbury, 1992.

"Gloria Houston." *Contemporary North Carolina Authors*, 1990.

Holtze, Sally Holmes. *Sixth Book of Junior Authors and Illustrators*. H. W. Wilson, 1989.

James, Elizabeth and Carol Barkin. *Sincerely Yours*. Clarion, 1993.

Kovacs, Deborah, and James Preller. *Meet the Authors and Illustrators*. Scholastic, 1991.

_____. *Meet the Authors and Illustrators*. Volume Two. Scholastic, 1993.

Levine, Michael. *The Kid's Address Book*. Perigee, 1992.

McElmeel, Sharon L. *An Author a Month (for Nickels)*. Libraries Unlimited, 1990.

_____. *An Author a Month (for Pennies)*. Libraries Unlimited, 1988.

_____. *Authors for Children: A Calendar*. Libraries Unlimited, 1992.

_____. *Bookpeople: A First Album*. Libraries Unlimited, 1990.

_____. *Bookpeople: A Multicultural Album*. Libraries Unlimited, 1992.

_____. *Bookpeople: A Second Album*. Libraries Unlimited, 1990.

Naylor, Phyllis Reynolds. *How I Came to Be a Writer*. Scholastic, 1987.

The Newbery and Caldecott Awards: A Guide to the Medal and Honor Books. American Library Association, 1992.

Rozakis, Laurie. *Meet the Author*. Troll, 1992.

Something About the Author Autobiography Series. Gale Research, 1986-.

Something About the Author. Gale Research, 1971-.

Watson, Lillian Eichler. *The Bantam Book of Correct Letter Writing*. Bantam, 1958.

Publisher Biographical Material

About Ann M. Martin. Scholastic, n.d.

About Daniel Cohen. Cobblehill, 1992.

About Natalie Kinsey-Warnock. Cobblehill, 1992.

Albert Whitman & Company Author Profile: David Patneaude. Whitman, n.d.

Anne Mazer. Knopf, n.d.

Ann M. Martin. Scholastic, 1991.

Ann McGovern. Scholastic, n.d.

Bantam & Dell/Delacorte Present Joan Lowery Nixon. Bantam Doubleday Dell, 1990.

Bantam & Dell Present Harry Mazer & Norma Fox Mazer. Bantam Doubleday Dell, 1990.

Bantam Books for Young Readers Presents Lurlene McDaniel. Bantam, n.d.

Bantam Doubleday Dell Presents Bijou Le Tord. Bantam Doubleday Dell, 1995.

Bantam Presents Caroline B. Cooney. Bantam Doubleday Dell, 1990.

Barbara Park. Knopf, n.d.

Ben Mikaelsen. Hyperion, n.d.

Bill Wallace. Holiday House, n.d.

Claudia Mills. Farrar Straus Giroux, 1997.

Constance C. Greene. Viking Puffin, 1990.
Cynthia DeFelice. Macmillan, 1992.
Debbie Dadey and Marcia Thornton Jones. Scholastic, n.d.
Doubleday Presents Daniel Cohen. Bantam Doubleday Dell, 1990.
Gail Gibbons. HarperCollins, 1992.
Gail Gibbons. Holiday House, 1991.
Get to Know Giles Laroche. Little Brown, 1992.
Get to Know Lee Bennett Hopkins. Little Brown, 1991.
Hans Wilhelm. Sterling, n.d.
James Cross Giblin. HarperCollins, 1993.
Jane Yolen. Harcourt Brace, n.d.
Jane Yolen. HarperCollins, n.d.
Jennifer Armstrong. Crown/Knopf, n.d.
Jim Aylesworth. Atheneum, 1992.
Johanna Hurwitz. Morrow, n.d.
Johanna Hurwitz. Scholastic, n.d.
Johanna Hurwitz. Viking Penguin, n.d.
Lee Bennett Hopkins. HarperCollins, 1992.
Leonard Everett Fisher. Holiday House, 1992.
Leonard Everett Fisher. Macmillan, 1992.
Liza Ketchum Murrow. Holiday House, n.d.
M. E. Kerr. HarperCollins, 1993.
Marianna Mayer. Macmillan, n.d.
Meet the Author Helena Clare Pittman. Carolrhoda, n.d.
Patricia C. McKissack From the Inside Out—The Author Speaks. Random House, n.d.
Peter Catalanotto. Orchard Books, 1992.
Peter Spier: Up Close and Personal. Doubleday, n.d.
Pleasant Company Introduces an American Girls Author: Janet Shaw. Pleasant Company, 1991.
Pleasant Company Introduces an American Girls Author: Valerie Tripp. Pleasant Company, 1997.
Puffin Profile: Betsy Byars. Puffin, n.d.
Suzy Kline. Putnam's, 1992.
Suzy Kline. Viking Puffin, 1990.
Theodore Taylor. Harcourt Brace, 1993.
Tom Birdseye. Holiday House, 1990.
Willo Davis Roberts. Atheneum, 1991.

Book Club Biographical Material

A Conversation with Jerry Spinelli. Arrow Book Club, 1991.
A Few Moments with Theodore Taylor. Tab Book Club, 1991.
Hopkins, Lee Bennett. *A Letter to the Class from Lee Bennett Hopkins.* The Trumpet Club, 1992.
Discovering Author Barbara Park. Weekly Reader Book Club, 1991.
Discovering Author Bill Wallace. Weekly Reader Book Club, 1992.
Discovering Author Eth Clifford. Weekly Reader Book Club, 1990.
Discovering Author Jane Yolen. Weekly Reader Book Club, 1992.
Elizabeth George Speare. The Trumpet Club, 1990.
Fritz, Jean. *A Letter to the Class from Jean Fritz.* The Trumpet Club, 1991.

▲▼▲

Phyllis Reynolds Naylor: The Trumpet Club Author Study Tape. The Trumpet Club, 1992.
Scholastic Salutes Elizabeth George Speare. Arrow Book Club, 1991.
Scholastic Salutes Jean Fritz. Arrow Book Club, 1991.
Stella Pevsner. Junior Library Guild, 1991.

Periodicals

Austin, Patricia. "Author and Illustrator Studies in the Classroom." *Book Links*, September, 1998.
"Author Spotlight: Rolling Through Life on My Bus." *Read*, January 29, 1993.
Brodie, Carolyn S. "Books and Videos About Children's Authors and Illustrators." *School Library Media Activities Monthly*, November 1992.
"Face-to-Face with Suzy Kline." *The Follett Forum*, Fall 1992.
Feldman, Roxanne Hsu. "Children's Book Authors and Illustrators on the Web." *Book Links*, September, 1998.
Horn, Chris. "The Middle Passage." *USC Times*, December 11, 1992.
Jones, Trev. *School Library Journal*, January 1994.
Krull, Kathleen. "Udder Voices, Udder Rooms." *New York Times Book Review*, November 14, 1993.
Martin, Ron. "Junior DISCovering Authors." *School Library Media Activities Monthly*, February 1995.
Miles, Betty. "When Children Write to Authors." *Learning90*, March, 1990.
Miller, Gloria, and Jo Sigmon. "So You Want to Place a Call to an Author/Illustrator." *School Library Media Activities Monthly*, November 1992.
Peary, Gerald. "Woman to Watch: Leslie Sills." *Boston Woman*, May 1989.
Phelan, Carolyn. "Reading the Mail—Books about Letters." *Book Links*, January 1992.
_____. "Writing the Mail—Letters in the Classroom." *Book Links*, July 1992.

Other Publications

Inviting Children's Book Authors and Illustrators to Your Community. The Children's Book Council, 1992.
James Lincoln Collier, Christopher Collier: Meet the Newbery Author Series. Random House, 1981.
New England Authors and Illustrators of Children's Books. New England Booksellers Association, 1992.
1993 Roster. Society of Children's Book Writers & Illustrators, 1993.
Publishers of Books for Young People. Society of Children's Book Writers & Illustrators, 1993.
SCBWI Guide to Agents. Society of Children's Book Writers & Illustrators, 1990.
Third-Class Mail Preparation. U.S. Postal Service, n.d.

▲▼▲

Photograph Credits

Note: All photographs are courtesy of the authors and illustrators themselves unless listed below.

Carol Adorjan - *Bill Dormin*
Thomas B. Allen - *Alan Ferguson*
Jennifer Armstrong - *Phil Haggerty*
Marion Dane Bauer - *Ann Goddard*
Jan Brett - *Orcutt Photography*
Larry Dane Brimmer - *Michael Hartung*
David Budbill - *Sargent N. Hill*
Betsy Byars - *Ed Byars*
Ann Cameron - *Das Anudas*
Christopher Collier - *Photography by Joseph*
Debbie Dadey - *Richard McFate*
Ed Emberley - *Steve Adams*
James Cross Giblin - *Miriam Berkley*
Mary Downing Hahn - *James Ferry Photography*
Patricia Hermes - *Robert Zuckerman*
Lee Bennett Hopkins - *Jeffrey Wein*
Gloria Houston - *John S. Payne Photography*
Johanna Hurwitz - *Amanda Smith*
Marcia Thornton Jones - *Tom Barnett*
M. E. Kerr - *Zoé Kamitses*
Liza Ketchum - *Janet Coleman*
Helen Ketteman - *Glamour Shots*

Marianna Mayer - *John Cane*
Anne Mazer - *Lindsay Barrett George*
Bijou Le Tord - *Lynda Sylvester*
Michael McCurdy - *Gerard Malanga*
Lurlene McDaniel - *Copeland Photography*
Ann McGovern - *Michael Ortiz*
Phyllis Reynolds Naylor - *Katherine Lambert*
Joan Lowery Nixon - *Kaye Marvins Photography*
Helena Clare Pittman - *Susan Gaber Barkey*
Berniece Rabe - *J. Malan Heslop*
Ronald Rood - *Jamie Cope*
Barbara Seuling - *Carol Stess*
Leslie Sills - *Thomas Lang*
Marilyn Singer - *Anthony Noel*
Peter Spier - *David Osika*
Barbara Steiner - *Avery*
Jane Sutton - *Alan Ticotsky*
Theodore Taylor - *John Graves*
Bill Wallace - *Carol Wallace*
Hans Wilhelm - *Anne Weber Mannheim*
Jane Yolen - *Jason Stemple*

Art Credits

From filmstrip *Murders in the Rue Morgue* by Leonard Everett Fisher ©1978. Used by permission.
Mouse in cheese locomotive by Matt Novak
Self-portrait by Keith Baker
Self-portrait by Ed Emberley
Students writing letters by Wendy Anderson Halperin
Pig by Arlene Dubanevich

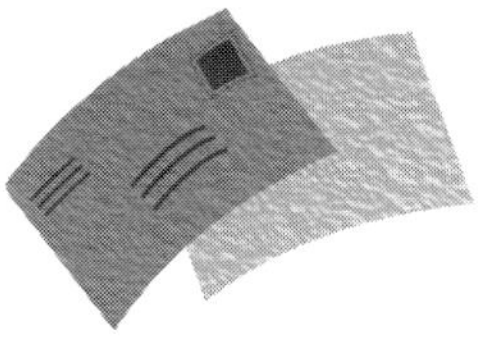

Additional Addresses of Authors and Illustrators